T0303289

Developing Outcome Measures for the National Guard Youth ChalleNGe Program

JENNIE W. WENGER, STEPHANI L. WRABEL, THOMAS E. TRAIL,
LOUAY CONSTANT, WING YI CHAN, KATHRYN A. EDWARDS, JOY S. MOINI,
HANNA HAN

Prepared for the Office of the Secretary of Defense
Approved for public release; distribution unlimited

RAND NATIONAL DEFENSE RESEARCH INSTITUTE

For more information on this publication, visit **www.rand.org/t/RRA271-5**.

Published by the RAND Corporation, Santa Monica, Calif.

Library of Congress Cataloging-in-Publication Data is available for this publication.

ISBN: 978-1-9774-0783-2

Cover: Wisconsin National Guard photo by Staff Sgt. Alex Baum.

About This Report

The National Guard Youth ChalleNGe program is a residential, quasi-military program for youth ages 16 to 18 who are experiencing difficulty in traditional high school. This report summarizes and documents findings and recommendations from analyses carried out between 2016 and 2020. The focus of this report is on determining how sites can measure their progress at meeting their overall mission ("to intervene in and reclaim the lives of 16- to 18-year-old high school dropouts, producing program graduates with the values, life skills, education, and self-discipline necessary to succeed as productive citizens").[1] Sources of data include information gathered during visits to each site, as well as site- and individual-level information gathered yearly over four years. We also use extant data sets and information from the existing literature as appropriate.

RAND National Security Research Division

This research was sponsored by the Office of the Assistant Secretary of Defense for Manpower and Reserve Affairs and conducted within the Forces and Resources Policy Center of the RAND National Security Research Division (NSRD), which operations the National Defense Research Institute (NDRI), a federally funded research and development center sponsored by the Office of the Secretary of Defense, the Joint Staff, the Unified Combatant Commands, the Navy, the Marine Corps, the defense agencies, and the defense intelligence enterprise.

For more information on the RAND Forces and Resources Policy Center, see www.rand.org/nsrd/frp or contact the director (contact information is provided on the webpage).

The research reported here was completed in August 2021 and underwent security review with the sponsor and the Defense Office of Prepublication and Security Review before public release.

Acknowledgments

We are grateful to the staff of the National Guard Youth ChalleNGe program. We thank the central administrative staff who assisted with many aspects of this research and the staff at each location who responded to our data requests in a timely fashion and provided detailed and thoughtful information during the course of our site visits. We are also grateful to our RAND colleagues for their support: Craig Bond and James Powers reviewed various portions

[1] The mission statement can be found on the ChalleNGe website (National Guard Youth ChalleNGe, undated), as well as in previous reports (see, for example, National Guard Youth ChalleNGe, 2015, p. 2). The mission statement appears to be widely shared across ChalleNGe sites. It is quoted in various materials and briefings used at the sites and was included in briefings that formed part of the site visits in past years.

of the report, and Emily Payne provided administrative support. We also thank Fadia Afashe for managing the publications process, as well as Samantha Bennett for carefully editing the report. Laura Miller of RAND and Jillian Berk of Mathematica Policy Research provided reviews to ensure that our work met RAND's high standards for quality. We thank all who contributed to this research or assisted with this report, but we retain full responsibility for the accuracy, objectivity, and analytical integrity of the work presented here.

Summary

The National Guard Youth ChalleNGe is a residential, quasi-military program for young people aged 16 to 18 who are experiencing academic difficulties and exhibiting problem behaviors inside and/or outside of school. ChalleNGe participants, known as *cadets*, may have dropped out of their previous high school, may have been in jeopardy of dropping out, and/or may have had run-ins with the criminal justice system. ChalleNGe's stated mission is "to intervene in and reclaim the lives of 16- to 18-year-old high school dropouts, producing program graduates with the values, life skills, education, and self-discipline necessary to succeed as productive citizens."[2] As such, the program is focused on creating opportunities for positive, long-term change.

As of early 2021, participating states operate 40 ChalleNGe sites through their state National Guard organizations with supporting federal funds and oversight.[3] Roughly 184,000 youth have successfully completed the program since it was established 25 years ago. Throughout the history of the program, sites have maintained records on the numbers of ChalleNGe applicants, entrants, and graduates, as well as information classifying the placement rates of recent graduates. Such data provide useful information to ChalleNGe staff and meet the reporting requirements placed on the program, but this information is not sufficient to determine how well the program is meeting its stated mission of creating long-term change and helping young people go on to become productive citizens.

Over the past four years, RAND Corporation researchers have worked closely with ChalleNGe policymakers and program staff to support two objectives: first, to gather and analyze existing data from each ChalleNGe site on an annual basis in support of the program's yearly reports to Congress; and, second, to develop approaches for measuring long-term outcomes, with a focus on understanding how well the program is doing at meeting its mission. In support of the first objective, the team developed a secure method of data collection, established a logic model of the ChalleNGe program, carried out visits to each site, and developed several research efforts, including a series of benchmarks using existing nationally representative data.[4] The focus of this report is the second objective—developing approaches for measuring

---

[2] The mission statement can be found on the ChalleNGe website (National Guard Youth ChalleNGe, undated), as well as in previous reports (see, for example, National Guard Youth ChalleNGe, 2015, p. 2). The mission statement appears to be widely shared across ChalleNGe sites.

[3] The number of sites changed over the course of this project. There were 40 sites as of early 2021, but there were most often 39 operational sites during the period when RAND researchers visited sites and collected most of the data reported here. Additionally, the ChalleNGe program includes five Job ChalleNGe sites.

[4] More information about these efforts can be found in our annual reports, additional reports, and in the later chapters of this report (see especially Wenger et al., 2017; Wenger, Constant, and Cottrell, 2018; Constant et al., 2019; Constant et al., 2020; and Edwards, 2020).

long-term outcomes that will allow officials of the program and the individual sites to understand the extent to which the program is meeting its mission.[5]

We used a mixed-methods approach to address this objective. Over the course of three and a half years, we collected and obtained data from many sources and used several analytic techniques as appropriate. This process included updates to the ChalleNGe logic model, data collection through site visits, annual data calls, and various analytic tasks and pilot projects. We used the information collected from the data sources above to develop recommendations to assist the ChalleNGe program in collecting data and measuring outcomes central to the program's mission.

ChalleNGe Program Design and Recent Trends

The ChalleNGe program emphasizes development of eight core components: leadership/followership, responsible citizenship, service to community, life-coping skills, physical fitness, health and hygiene, job skills, and academic excellence. The program is 17.5 months in length and includes a two-week acclimation period, followed by a five-month residential phase and a 12-month post-residential phase. The latter phase provides time for graduates to continue their education, find employment, enlist in the military, or take part in some combination of these activities. Each graduate has a volunteer mentor from the cadet's home community who provides advice, assists with the transition after ChalleNGe, and provides monthly reports to the program about the graduate's placement (i.e., education, employment, military).

There is some past evidence that ChalleNGe is effective at meeting at least some aspects of its mission to create long-term change in participants. The main source of evidence for overall program effectiveness derives from a randomized controlled trial (RCT) run in the mid-2000s (Bloom, Gardenhire-Crooks, and Mandsager, 2009) that included a limited number of ChalleNGe sites. The findings indicate that the ChalleNGe program had positive impacts on educational and labor market outcomes.[6] Additionally, a separate study found that the life-coping skills stressed in ChalleNGe appeared to increase participants' noncognitive or social and emotional skills (Malone and Atkin, 2016), and the relationship between social and

[5] We note that, although we recommend outcomes for sites to measure, we do not propose specific long-term metrics at this point owing to variation in sites' resources and capabilities to support data collection and the lack of a central program administrative database that would support systemization and consistency in data collection and measurement.

[6] An RCT, considered the gold standard within social science research, compares outcomes for two groups: a *treatment* group (in this case, a group of applicants who were accepted into the ChalleNGe program) and a *control* group (a similar group of young people who were not admitted into the ChalleNGe program). Randomization between the treatment and control groups is a key requirement for an RCT to establish baseline equivalence between the two groups; with randomization, any differences between the groups can then be attributed to the ChalleNGe program.

emotional skills and long-term outcomes is well established (see, e.g., Durlak et al., 2011; and Dweck, Walton, and Cohen, 2014).

In terms of recent trends, during the 2015–2018 period, a typical site had about 150 entrants to each class, of which about 120 cadets graduated from ChalleNGe (about 80 percent). The average numbers of entrants and graduates decreased slightly over this period, and spending on ChalleNGe sites increased slightly. The increase in costs is far lower than increases in most postsecondary institutions, and much of the increase is related to opening new programs. Finally, the costs per participant and per graduate remain modest when compared with other youth programs (Wenger et al., 2017).

Gaps in Existing Data Collection

ChalleNGe sites currently collect considerable data; they have detailed information on the number of applicants, entrants, and graduates, as well as on other relevant outcomes, such as the amount of community service performed. All sites also keep data on standardized test scores and other measures of academic progress; sites gather placement data through mentors. Sites adhere to existing policies about data collection and reporting.

However, current data collection is not sufficient, in either scope or period of time covered, to support measurement of long-term outcomes. Placement data generally include no more than 12 months of information, and sites frequently express concern that mentor reporting drops off sharply after graduation. Placement information includes only minimal detail about the placement. For example, sites may not be able to document industry or occupation, existence of benefits, or even total earnings.

Unlike many large, national programs, the ChalleNGe program does not keep a single, authoritative administrative database, although each site does collect data as required, and many of the sites use a similar database, the Cadet Tracker. Centralized tracking and analysis require data to be collected from individual sites. RAND researchers have collected consistent data for the past four years, and the National Guard Bureau also collects data periodically. Beyond these *data calls*, some sites have tested other methods of data collection, including development of a customized database and use of contractor support to track graduate placement.

Recommendations

Measuring the extent to which ChalleNGe is meeting its mission will require collection of additional information—better measures of the quality of the process indicators, such as measures of contact hours, cadet engagement and learning in the classroom, and information documenting graduates' long-term outcomes. We note, however, that there is no single, uniform answer to the question of how sites should approach determining success at meeting their mission. This is the case because, despite a strong model with a series of core components, there are substantive and important differences across the sites. Some stem from the circumstances in the states and communities in which the sites are located; others stem from the sites' approaches to data collection, storage, staff capacity, budget, etc. To accommodate this variation, our recommendations are stringent enough to allow sites to develop a better understanding of their success at meeting their mission while being flexible enough to work with different sites' various approaches.

Each site should select the data collection strategy or strategies most appropriate to the site context. There are several major strategies for collecting information on graduates: collect information from all graduates on an ongoing basis by maintaining contact with them postgraduation; periodically survey graduates; or use existing information in state- or national-level databases to measure outcomes. Depending on the site's limitations and resources, a strategy that combines several approaches may be most appropriate, especially in the short run.

Surveys offer an option for collecting information on long-term outcomes that is not included in regular data collection efforts. However, we note that surveying alumni raises several issues—first, the site must locate the alumni (or advertise on a platform that they are likely to see); second, most surveys have low response rates, and thus responses may not be generalizable without weighting or other advanced statistical techniques. Finally, matching the responses to the administrative data and analyzing the results are not trivial activities; in nearly every case, ChalleNGe sites lack the technical expertise and the resources required to complete the analyses.

Another option is to organize ChalleNGe staff during defined periods to focus on data collection related to long-term outcomes—for example, by assigning an employee to take on this responsibility or to contract for analytic support. As individual ChalleNGe sites consider their strategies, the existence and accessibility of national- and state-level data sets may influence their decisions.

Regardless of the strategy used to collect information, being able to store and, more importantly, access and analyze the data collected requires a database of some form. Without consideration of resource requirements, collecting long-term information on all graduates (or perhaps on all participants) and storing the information in a user-friendly database is preferable to other strategies. But this approach may not be practical for all sites.

The optimal strategy may change over time. For example, a site may decide to survey current graduates for immediate information on long-term outcomes but also to put in place a strategy and the resources required to maintain contact with all graduates going forward.

All sites should discuss the importance of data collection with cadets and parents. However each site decides to collect information, we recommend that all sites share and explain the data collection to cadets and parents (and continue to socialize these efforts with mentors). Sites should communicate the importance of data collection efforts and could also consider appropriate incentives for graduates, parents, or mentors who keep in contact. In general, improving mentor engagement will be helpful to these efforts.

Site and program staff should budget for data collection now. Long-term outcome data can be collected in a variety of ways, but all approaches will require resources. We recommend that site/program staff begin to plan and budget for this effort now, and we expect that, in many cases, the amount budgeted should be considerably more than the salary or time of one staff member. A first step would be to identify specific long-term outcome measures, identify preferred methods to collect the information, and begin to form an estimate in terms of staff time and other resources required.

All sites should collect, at a minimum, data on graduates' educational attainment, labor force experience, and progress on other core components. We recommend that all sites collect specific information on educational attainment (completion of the General Educational Development certificate, completion of a high school diploma, completion of standard industry-recognized certificates or similar credentials, and completion of college courses/programs). We also recommend collecting specific information on labor force experience—hours worked, pay, job turnover, existence of benefits, and industry and occupation. These recommendations stem from the fact that the long-term positive effects of ChalleNGe are driven by increases in educational attainment and earnings. In addition, we recommend collecting information to track progress in the other core components, e.g., family formation, civic participation, health and well-being. Comparing outcomes with benchmarks described in Edwards, 2020, may help sites contextualize and assess progress.

Sites should collect data for three years postgraduation. Collecting information over a three-year postgraduation period would allow time for many graduates to continue or complete their education and to settle into the job market. However, if staff find that most graduates have not yet completed their education at the end of the three-year window, then tracking graduates for a longer period may be advisable.

The ChalleNGe program should invest in a single, consistent administrative database. Our final recommendation is that the ChalleNGe program invest in a single, consistent administrative database. Such a system would allow consistent data collection and reporting and could result in substantial increases in efficiency, quality, and usability.

We recognize that this option would represent a substantial upfront cost, as well as some ongoing costs, but it offers substantial advantages, including automatically generated reports at the site and program levels and easier matching of ChalleNGe data with existing data in state or national systems. Over time, a well-populated administrative database could provide the information needed to select a random subsample of graduates for a focused survey or for a panel to be contacted periodically to learn more about their experiences. The Cadet Tracker database may offer a model for a program-wide database. However, we recommend that, prior to determining how to standardize data collection, program staff assess Cadet Tracker's weaknesses and limitations as well as its strengths and understand why some sites do not use the system.

Finally, any national database would need strong security features. We recognize that the ChalleNGe program must meet myriad data requirements; some of these requirements are relevant given the U.S. Department of Defense's oversight, but state requirements differ—

and, in general, programs that include minor participants face strict data security requirements. An off-the-shelf system could offer some advantages in terms of technical support.

Closing Thoughts

The ChalleNGe program remains well-focused to serve young people who struggle in traditional high schools. At this point, the program lacks systematic measures of graduates' long-term progress; without such measures, both documenting progress in meeting the program's mission and making necessary improvements are not possible.

Contents

Figures and Tables

Figures

Tables

CHAPTER ONE

Introduction

The National Guard Youth ChalleNGe program, established in the mid-1990s, is a residential, quasi-military program for young people who are experiencing difficulties or exhibiting problematic behaviors in or outside of school. ChalleNGe participants may have dropped out of their previous high school, may have been in jeopardy of dropping out, and/or may have had run-ins with the criminal justice system. ChalleNGe's stated mission is "to intervene in and reclaim the lives of 16- to 18-year-old high school dropouts, producing program graduates with the values, life skills, education, and self-discipline necessary to succeed as productive citizens."[1] Accordingly, the program is focused on creating opportunities for positive, long-term change.

As of early 2021, participating states operate 40 sites through their state National Guard organizations with supporting federal funds and oversight; additionally, Job ChalleNGe sites provided flexible, residential job-training programs for participants in six states.[2] ChalleNGe sites vary in size, but, to date, nearly 250,000 young people have enrolled in ChalleNGe, and roughly 184,000 have successfully completed the program. The National Guard is responsible for all day-to-day operation of ChalleNGe, while the Office of the Secretary of Defense provides oversight and policy guidance.

Throughout the history of the program, sites have maintained records on the numbers of ChalleNGe applicants, entrants, and graduates, as well as information classifying the placement rates of recent graduates. Such data provide useful information to ChalleNGe staff and meet the reporting requirements placed on the program, but this information is not sufficient to determine how well the program is meeting its stated mission of creating long-term change and helping young people go on to become productive citizens.

Over the past four years, RAND Corporation researchers have worked closely with ChalleNGe policymakers and program staff to support two objectives: first, to gather and analyze existing data from each ChalleNGe site on an annual basis in support of the program's yearly

---

[1] The mission statement can be found on the ChalleNGe website (National Guard Youth ChalleNGe, undated).

[2] Job ChalleNGe sites are located in California, Georgia, Louisiana, Michigan, South Carolina, and West Virginia; the Louisiana site is funded through the U.S. Department of Labor. ChalleNGe sites are present in 31 states and territories (including the District of Columbia and Puerto Rico). Several states have multiple programs.

reports to Congress; and, second, to develop approaches for measuring long-term outcomes, with a focus on understanding how well the program is doing at meeting its mission. In support of the first objective, the team developed a secure method of data collection, established a logic model of the ChalleNGe program, carried out visits to each site, and developed several research efforts, including a series of benchmarks using existing nationally representative data.[3] The focus of this report is the second objective—developing approaches for measuring long-term outcomes that will allow the program and the individual sites to understand the extent to which the program is meeting its mission.

We note that, while we aim in this report to provide approaches and recommendations to support measurement of long-term outcomes, we do not provide a list of specific long-term metrics that all sites should use. There is tremendous variation across ChalleNGe sites in terms of available resources and capabilities; as a result, there is no single, uniform answer to the question of how sites should approach determining success at meeting their mission. Some differences across sites stem from the circumstances in the states and communities in which the sites are located; others stem from the sites' approaches to data collection, storage, staff capacity, budget, etc. To accommodate this variation, we recommend approaches for long-term data collection that sites can adapt to their specific circumstances.

In the remainder of this introduction, we provide an overview of the ChalleNGe program and then describe the approach used to examine current data collection and develop our recommendations.

Overview of ChalleNGe

The ChalleNGe program is organized around eight core components: academic excellence, leadership/followership, responsible citizenship, service to community, life-coping skills, physical fitness, health and hygiene, and job skills. Daily schedules include substantial amounts of time for classroom instruction and studying, but cadets also take part in a variety of other activities that focus on physical fitness, teamwork, and service to community. Sites may also include a variety of other activities, such as cadet clubs or occasional field trips. Graduation requires participating in and completing all activities, but it does not depend on any specific academic requirements (such as achieving a score on a standardized test or completing a set number of high school credits).

The program is 17.5 months in length and is made up of a 5.5-month residential phase followed by a 12-month post-residential phase. Each participant, or *cadet*, has a mentor whose role is to provide advice and assist with the transition to additional education or employment. While cadets interact with their mentors during the residential phase, the mentors'

---

3 More information about these efforts can be found in our annual reports, additional reports, and in the later chapters of this report (see, especially, Wenger et al., 2017; Wenger, Constant, and Cottrell, 2018; Constant et al., 2019; Constant et al., 2020; Wenger et al., 2021; and Edwards, 2020; and Edwards, Zaber, and Schwam, 2022).

role becomes more focused during the post-residential phase as mentors meet regularly with cadets and provide monthly reports on graduate placement (i.e., education, employment, or military enlistment) to staff at the ChalleNGe site.

Program Effectiveness

The majority of ChalleNGe graduates have at least one academic credential at the end of the program, and graduates have performed over 12 million hours of community service while enrolled. In a typical year, more than 12,000 young people enroll at a ChalleNGe site, and nearly 10,000 graduate.[4] Roughly 70 percent of the young people who are not on track to complete high school live in states with a ChalleNGe program; the overall size of this group is approximately 1.4 million.[5]

There is some past evidence that ChalleNGe is effective at meeting at least some aspects of its mission to create long-term change in participants. The main source of evidence for overall program effectiveness derives from a randomized controlled trial (RCT) run in the mid-2000s that included a limited number of ChalleNGe sites. The findings indicate that the ChalleNGe program had positive impacts on educational and labor market outcomes.[6] The study measured outcomes over a three-year period; at the end of three years, cadets included in the RCT had completed more postsecondary education and were more likely to be working than similar young people who did not take part in ChalleNGe.[7]

---

4 These numbers include all who entered ChalleNGe during 1993–2019. RAND researchers are currently collecting data on the 2020 cadets; this information will be published in a report in early 2022. We present additional information on trends across ChalleNGe in Chapter Three. For more detailed information on classes in recent years, see Wenger et al., 2017; Wenger, Constant, and Cottrell, 2018; Constant et al., 2019; Constant et al. 2020; and Wenger et al., 2021.

5 This estimate uses the adjusted cohort graduation rate (ACGR), a statistic measuring the proportion of public school students who attain a regular high school diploma within four years of entering ninth grade (see National Center for Education Statistics, 2019). The most recent estimates are that 84 percent of ninth graders in the United States will receive a diploma within four years and that 16 percent will not. We use state-level estimates from the ACGR and the youth population to estimate the number who are and are not on track. ACGR data are not available for Puerto Rico; we assume the average ACGR for students in Puerto Rico. Note that ACGR rates are lower among students from historically marginalized racial/ethnic groups; see Common Core of Data, 2018.

6 An RCT, considered the gold standard within social science research, compares outcomes for two groups: a *treatment* group (in this case, a group of applicants who were accepted into the ChalleNGe program) and a *control* group (a similar group of young people who were not admitted into the ChalleNGe program). Randomization between the treatment and control groups is a key requirement for an RCT to establish baseline equivalence between the two groups; with randomization, any differences between the groups can then be attributed to the ChalleNGe program.

7 While ChalleNGe was found to have a positive effect on most educational and labor market outcomes, negative effects or no effects were found on several outcomes that might be expected to differ among participants and nonparticipants. There was no difference in arrest rates, and participants were somewhat more likely than others to be overweight at the end of the three-year period (Millenky et al., 2011).

Additionally, a separate study found that the life-coping skills stressed in ChalleNGe appear to increase participants' noncognitive or social and emotional skills (Malone and Atkin, 2016), and the relationship between social and emotional skills and long-term outcomes is well established (see, among others, Durlak et al., 2011; and Dweck, Walton, and Cohen, 2014). The relationships among many other aspects of the core components and long-term outcomes are less well established, but there is evidence of the effectiveness of mentoring, especially when the mentoring relationship is structured as it is within ChalleNGe.[8]

The labor market outcomes of ChalleNGe participants are impressive when compared with studies of other programs aimed at high school dropouts, and the outcomes are perhaps even more impressive given inadvertent timing. The RCT of ChalleNGe described by Millenky et al., 2011, took place during the severe economic recession whose effects were particularly pronounced on young workers with minimal amounts of education. A separate, careful analysis of all costs and benefits based on the outcomes from the RCT found ChalleNGe to be cost-effective, producing approximately $2.66 in benefits (appropriately discounted) for each $1.00 invested (Perez-Arce et al., 2012). This cost-benefit analysis is based on longer-term educational and labor market outcomes than most sites collect (the RCT measured outcomes for three years).

Thus, there is strong evidence of both ChalleNGE's effectiveness and cost-effectiveness—but the evidence is somewhat outdated and is based on a subset of the program sites. In addition, there is *no* evidence that the program has become less effective over time; indeed, as more sites have offered high school credits and occupation-specific training, the program's effectiveness may have increased. However, current guidelines require that sites collect information on ChalleNGe graduates' placement for only 12 months after graduation. Therefore, most sites do *not* collect the information that would be necessary to confirm that the program is meeting its mission and having a longer-term influence on participants.

Study Approach

As noted earlier, this report is part of a multiyear study of the ChalleNGe program. The two primary objectives of the entire research project were (1) to gather and analyze consistent, existing data from each ChalleNGe site and (2) to develop approaches for measuring long-term outcomes, with a focus on understanding how well the program is doing at meeting its mission. To meet the first objective, we collected data from each site in 2016, 2017, 2018, 2019, and 2020. Results and analyses from each wave of data collection are documented in our annual reports (Wenger et al., 2017; Wenger, Constant, and Cottrell, 2018; Constant et al., 2019; Constant et al., 2020; Wenger et al., 2021).

---

[8] The ChalleNGe youth-initiated mentoring model is linked to more-enduring relationships between the cadet and the mentor, especially among cadets who select the mentors themselves. See Schwartz et al., 2013. For more information on the effects of mentoring across various interventions, see Rhodes, Spencer, et al., 2006; Tierney, Grossman, and Resch, 2000; and Resnjanskij et al., 2021.

To meet the second objective, which is the focus of this report, we used a multi-methods approach. Over the course of three and a half years, we collected and obtained data from many different sources and used several analytic techniques, as appropriate.

Logic Model

To guide our thinking about how ChalleNGe works and how to go about measuring program outcomes, we developed a *logic model* at the beginning of the study to clarify the reasoning behind the program's structure and activities. Logic models illustrate the ways in which programs could be expected to produce outcomes in the short, medium, and long terms. Logic models also are helpful in identifying the broader community-based effects that might arise from a program.[9] Therefore, a logic model can serve as a blueprint for evaluating the program's effectiveness.

Data Collection

Informed by the logic model, we next collected data through multiple mechanisms, including site visits, annual data calls, and various analytic tasks and pilot projects.

We visited each program site at least once throughout the course of this project. We requested basic data, such as the organization chart, weekly schedule, and the site's outreach briefing, from the sites prior to each visit. We toured each site and used a semistructured list of questions to guide our conversations with key staff members. The resulting qualitative data provided information about many aspects of the program, as well as site-specific innovations and challenges. We used the information gathered on these *site visits* to inform our annual data calls and the analytic tasks and pilot projects described below.

We requested and received data from each ChalleNGe site on an annual basis. The core data collected remained generally consistent across years. The information from these *annual data calls* forms the basis of our inputs to the program's annual report to Congress; these data also allowed us to explore specific aspects of the program. We collected site-level information, such as funding and staffing levels, dates of classes, and number of applicants. We also collected cadet-level information on standardized test scores, program completion, and eventual post-residential placements. Collecting consistent data at the site and the individual levels over the course of the study allows analysis and reporting of trends; without such data, it is possible to report aggregated trends (for example, the total number of participants, total cost, and average cost per participant), but it is not possible to report more-sophisticated analyses (such as average cost per participant at established sites). Such trend analyses pro-

[9] For a useful primer on logic models, see Knowlton and Phillips, 2009.

vide valuable information to program decisionmakers; each annual report includes trend analyses.[10]

While RAND's annual data calls provide the information required to produce an annual report to Congress, these data calls do not include all data that the programs collect. We also collected detailed information from each ChalleNGe site on the types of data the site collects and stores. Understanding the data that sites currently possess helped to ensure the relevance of our conclusions and recommendations.

As appropriate, we drew on *extant data*, such as national samples matching the profile of ChalleNGe cadets. For example, we used data based on the Census as well as information collected by the National Center for Education Statistics to describe the target population of young people. We used data from nationally representative longitudinal surveys to understand the range of outcomes among young people who do not participate in ChalleNGe. We also consulted published literature in several relevant areas.

Analyses and Pilot Projects

We designed and carried out several *analytic tasks* and two *pilot projects* in close collaboration with individual ChalleNGe sites. For the purpose of this report, we describe analytic tasks that use information from multiple ChalleNGe sites as *research efforts*, while *pilot projects* are efforts that involve working closely with a single site to implement a trial program according to best practices. The results of the pilot projects have implications for many or all ChalleNGe sites. We describe the results of some of these efforts in separate documents (Edwards, 2020; Corte and Sontag-Padilla, 2021) but also include details from a pilot project to survey graduates in Appendix E.

Development of Recommendations

We used the information collected from the data sources above to develop recommendations to assist the ChalleNGe program in collecting data and measuring outcomes central to the program's mission.

Our logic model provided a framework for understanding how ChalleNGe would be expected to bring about change, as well as a breakdown of potential outcome measures in the short, medium, and long terms. Site visits allowed us to deepen our knowledge of the program's activities, learn more about the data that sites collected, and better understand the influence of external factors. Based on conversations with sites, we launched a data inventory to better understand existing data and gaps. Comparing outcomes that would be expected

[10] We note that annual data calls are necessary because ChalleNGe does not keep a single, authoritative administrative database. Many, but not all, of the sites do use an Access database called Cadet Tracker. Establishing such a database would create opportunities to collect additional data, but such a change would also present challenges. We discuss a variety of data-related possibilities in the last two chapters.

according to the logic model with the types of information sites currently collect suggested unevenness in terms of site-level data collection.

We also drew on extant data collected throughout the project; our benchmarks report (Edwards, 2020), which uses data from nationally representative surveys to understand outcomes among all young people, is an especially salient example.[11] We used data and information from analytic tasks and pilot projects as necessary; in particular, a pilot project to collect survey data on ChalleNGe graduates from one site provided practical lessons learned about the possibilities and limitations of surveying ChalleNGe participants. Finally, we searched existing information to better understand how other youth programs measure outcomes and to identify relevant existing scales and measures that span the inventory of potentially relevant outcomes.

Organization of This Report

The remainder of this report is organized as follows:

- In Chapter Two, we document the design of ChalleNGe, including the program's original impetus and mission, and describe the program's logic model and its role in helping us to better understand the program's mechanisms, structure, and activities.
- In Chapter Three, we provide a review of program trends. These data provide an overview of what is known about the program, which will help establish a foundation for the discussion of program measurement.
- In Chapter Four, we present a review of currently available data collected by programs, including some examples of how these data can be leveraged to more richly conceptualize program performance and site-specific needs and successes.
- In Chapter Five, we discuss several approaches for tracking long-term outcomes and recommend some outcomes to measure.
- In Chapter Six, we provide conclusions and recommendations for the ChalleNGe program and for individual sites. The goal of the recommendations is to assist the ChalleNGe program in providing richer, more-detailed reporting on participants' longer-term outcomes.

The report also contains five appendixes. Appendix A describes contextual factors that influence ChalleNGe sites. Appendix B presents how some similar youth programs approach data collection and outcomes measurement. Appendix C describes some potential measures of citizenship, leadership/followership, and service to community. Appendix D presents results from a pilot program aimed at increasing support for mentors. Appendix E describes

[11] This report is aimed at program staff to help them understand outcomes—for example, the report indicates how expected levels of education, earnings, family formation, and arrest rates of participants compare with outcomes of others who did not complete high school.

results from a survey of Washington Youth Academy (WYA) and provides additional information about how we analyzed the survey data.

CHAPTER TWO

ChalleNGe: Program Design and Logic Model

Although ChalleNGe operates on a strong and well-developed model (see the Donohue model, discussed in Price, 2010), program sites are located across the United States and, thus, are influenced by their communities and operate within a local context. Despite this variation, all sites incorporate a set of core program elements that are intended to meet program goals.

In this chapter, we first describe the central features of the ChalleNGe program and then use a logic model to map out the program's structure, resources, activities, outputs, and outcomes. A logic model is useful for clarifying the relationship between program activities and expected results and, thus, helps us understand how the program influences participants through the flow of inputs, processes or activities, expected outputs, and expected outcomes. After presenting the logic model, we look at the outcomes currently collected by ChalleNGe sites to identify potential areas for future measurement, which will be discussed at more length later in the report.

Design of ChalleNGe

The ChalleNGe program is designed as an immersive, quasi-military youth corps with a focus on the whole person.[1] The ChalleNGe program developed in response to a growing recognition of the relationship between educational attainment and job earnings. Beginning around the late 1970s, the returns on a college degree increased in the United States, while wages for those with no high school diploma fell, and middle-class blue-collar jobs became much more scarce (see, e.g., Katz and Autor, 1999; Autor, Levy, and Murnane, 2003; Tüzemen and Willis, 2013). Many factors could have at least some role in explaining these changes; the combination of factors resulted in a sharp increase in earnings inequality (see, among others, Bound and Johnson, 1995; Acemoglu, 2002). In short, getting ahead now required at least a high school diploma, and often additional education or training was necessary.

[1] For a description of the journey from idea to program, see Price, 2010.

In 1990, researchers at the Center for Strategic and International Studies developed a new approach for young people who had become disengaged from high school or who had left school without a diploma. This approach formed the basis for the National Guard Youth ChalleNGe program.

ChalleNGe differed from existing programs in several ways. First, ChalleNGe was designed as a statewide residential program run on a quasi-military model, rather than as a smaller and more targeted intervention run through specific schools or communities. But ChalleNGe's focus on the *whole person* model was perhaps even more radical, with the program designed as a broad intervention to help participants develop skills and positive habits across a wide range of areas. The program certainly bears some resemblance to the older Job Corps program, but the architects of ChalleNGe viewed the combination of addressing underlying factors rather than focusing on surface behaviors *and* using aspects of the military experience as crucial ingredients to assure ChalleNGe's success.

The ChalleNGe model includes eight core components:[2]

- academic excellence (all cadets attend academic classes on a daily basis)
- leadership/followership (the program provides a variety of roles for cadets)
- responsible citizenship (addressed through classroom and practical experiences)
- service to community (all cadets participate in substantial volunteer opportunities)
- life-coping skills (the program focuses on developing discipline and coping skills)
- physical fitness (cadets participate in physical training throughout the program)
- health and hygiene (the program emphasizes many aspects of physical and mental well-being)
- job skills (programs use a variety of activities to accomplish career exploration).

Additionally, ChalleNGe featured a substantial follow-up component: All participants had a mentor, and the mentor-mentee relationship was designed to last at least a year after the end of the program.

The program was initially piloted in 1990 and judged successful; as of early 2021, there were 40 sites in 28 states, the District of Columbia, and Puerto Rico. The program is open to individuals aged 16 to 18 who have dropped out of high school or who are not on track to graduate; participants must be drug-free and must enter the program voluntarily. The Secretary of Defense has responsibility for policy and budget oversight for the program (32 U.S.C. 509). Program sites are operated with input from the Department of Defense (DoD), the state (or district or territory), and the National Guard Bureau. A cooperative agreement spells out many of the operational details of the program.

The program is structured as follows. Those taking part in ChalleNGe enter as a group. The residential phase of the program lasts for 22 weeks. The first two weeks are referred to as the *pre-ChalleNGe* or *acclimation* phase; this phase serves as an orientation and includes an emphasis on physical conditioning, discipline, teamwork, and military bearing. Participants (who are generally referred to as *cadets*) next enter 20 weeks of a structured curriculum,

[2] For more information on the core components and the Donohue interventional model, see Price, 2010.

which is centered on the program's eight core components. This phase includes intensive classroom work and physical training; volunteer activities; extracurricular activities, such as sports and clubs; field trips; and various opportunities for teamwork and leadership. Along with instructors, administrators, counselors, and others, ChalleNGe program sites employ staff who work with and monitor cadets around the clock; these staff members are referred to as *cadre*.

All cadets select a mentor (or have one assigned if they cannot find one on their own).[3] Mentors and cadets are expected to meet regularly for at least 12 months after the cadet leaves the residential phase of ChalleNGe; this *post-residential* period is viewed as a key window for cadets to carry out the plans that they develop during the residential phase. The program uses a document called a Post-Residential Action Plan to provide structure and assist with planning: Cadets may plan to continue or complete their education, enter the labor force, enter the military, or undertake other activities. Mentors also play a key role in providing information to the ChalleNGe sites: Mentors are charged with reporting graduates' educational and employment-related activities each month. Although sites have other methods of gaining information on cadets' activities, mentors are the primary source of this information. Therefore, maintaining mentor engagement is a necessary step to measuring program and cadet success in the post-residential period.

Recently, ChalleNGe added a Job ChalleNGe program, which provides additional structure and training for ChalleNGe graduates. Job ChalleNGe is a residential program lasting 5.5 months. ChalleNGe graduates may enter Job ChalleNGe immediately after graduation or at a later point. Job ChalleNGe began in 2017 as a three-year pilot program at three sites; the program was funded jointly by DoD, the Department of Justice, and the Department of Labor. As of early 2020, Job ChalleNGe was operating in California, Georgia, Louisiana, Michigan, South Carolina, and West Virginia.[4]

A Logic Model for ChalleNGe

ChalleNGe is designed to influence a broad range of outcomes, including labor force participation, civic participation, and aspects of physical health. The program's eight core components are woven through ChalleNGe's curricula, and the interconnectedness of the program's core components is posited to be at the center of the program's capacity to produce change.

We developed a logic model to describe how the program structure and activities are expected to generate the intended outcomes. Such a model specifies the reasoning behind

[3] Program sites assign mentors when the cadet cannot find an adult who is appropriate to serve in this role, but in most cases the mentor is youth-initiated (this model is sometimes referred to as a *warm match*). See Rhodes, Spencer, et al., 2006, and Tierney, Grossman, and Resch, 2000.

[4] The Department of Labor provides funding for the Louisiana Job ChalleNGe site; the other Job ChalleNGe sites are funded primarily by DoD, but the states also provide some funding. This DoD/state funding pattern is similar to the pattern used to fund the ChalleNGe sites.

program structure and activities, as well as how those activities are connected to expected program results (Knowlton and Phillips, 2009). Over the course of this study (2016–2020), we expanded and clarified much of our knowledge and understanding around how ChalleNGe programs operate and what they offer to cadets and graduates. Based on this learning, we revised the ChalleNGe logic model (which had been first presented in Wenger et al., 2017), updating the model to more accurately reflect current ChalleNGe program functioning. The logic model was refined to more accurately

- reflect the diversity in inputs, activities, outputs, and outcomes of ChalleNGe sites across the country
- depict the importance of recruitment and application activities for sites
- ensure that all eight core components are represented in program outputs and outcomes in ways that are measurable
- reflect the influence that individual-level cadet changes have on community, government, and military outcomes in the short, medium, and long terms.

The revised logic model continues to emphasize the temporal aspects of the ChalleNGe program and its influence on participants by detailing the inputs, processes or activities, expected outputs, and expected outcomes of ChalleNGe for graduates, the communities where graduates reside, and the military.[5] Figure 2.1 displays the revised logic model, and we next describe the inputs, activities, outputs, and outcomes in the model.

Inputs

The inputs include policy and planning resources that guide the implementation of ChalleNGe's national strategy at the local level and enable individual sites to provide academic instruction and job training to cadets. Program assets are the resources that provide the capacity for program operation.

Activities

To reflect the different activities that ChalleNGe sites undertake across a program cycle, we grouped program activities into three phases: recruitment and application, acclimation, and residential. The post-residential phase of ChalleNGe overlaps with program outputs (e.g., cadets graduate from ChalleNGe) and short-term outcomes (e.g., graduates placed in school,

[5] Program logic models are a useful way of specifying the reasoning behind program structure and activities, as well as how those activities are connected to expected program results (Knowlton and Phillips, 2009). They are used to illustrate how program resources, activities, services (inputs), and direct products of services (outputs) are designed to produce short-term, medium-term, and long-term outcomes. Logic models also identify broader community effects that should result from program activities and services (Knowlton and Phillips, 2009). In this way, these models can communicate how a program contributes not only to the specific needs and outcomes of participants but also to the broader community and society at large. Program logic models also serve as a blueprint for evaluating how effectively a program is meeting its expected goals.

FIGURE 2.1
National Guard Youth ChalleNGe Logic Model

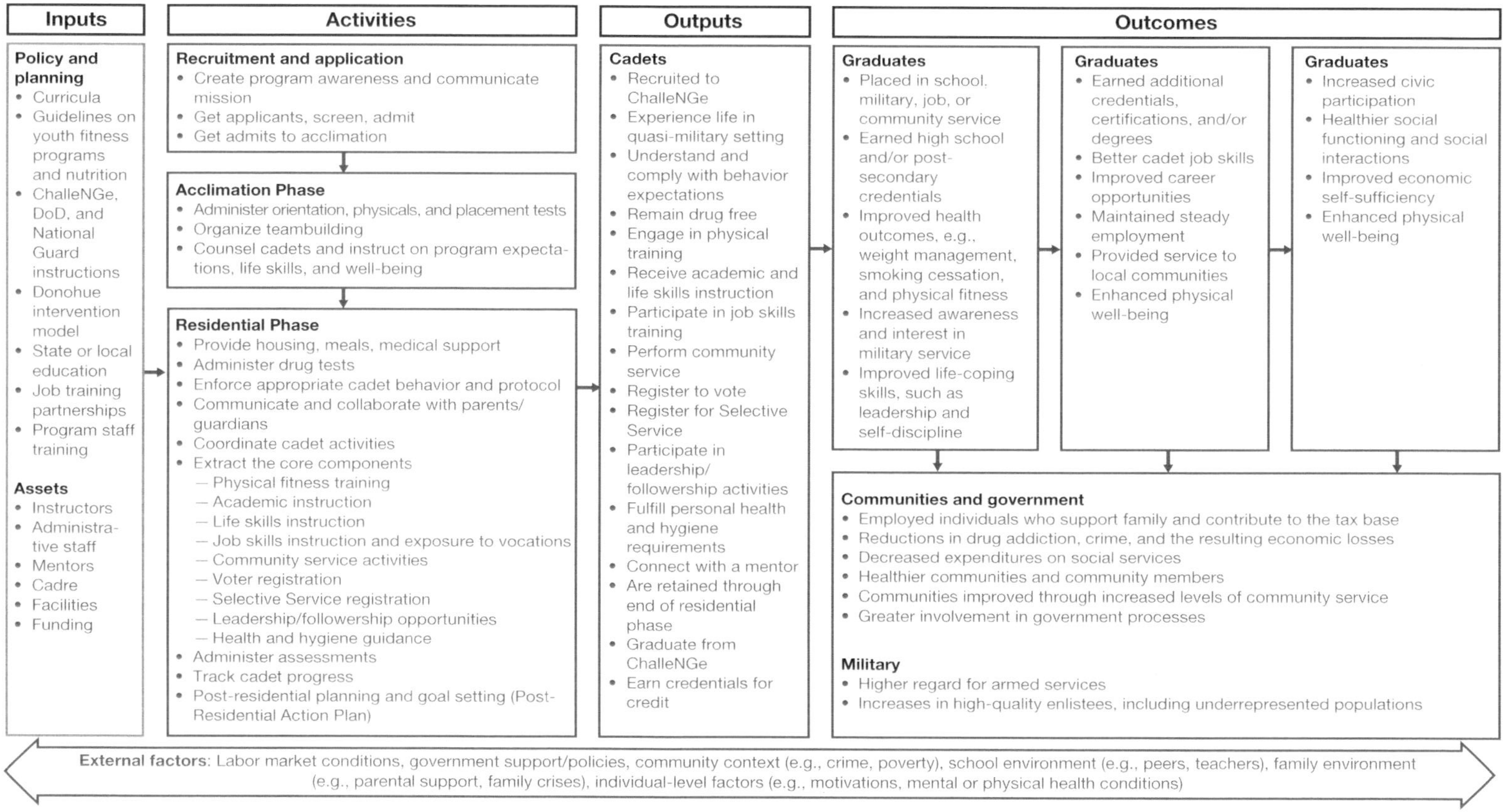

SOURCE: See Wenger et al., 2017, for discussion of development and original version of the model. Model has been refined based on discussions with program staff.

military, job, or community service). Activities that sites engage in to monitor graduates and to support mentors and graduates in the post-residential period are included in the residential phase activities.

Recruitment and Application

During the recruitment and application phase, recruiters conduct visits to schools, juvenile justice programs, or other relevant points of contact to create awareness of the program and communicate ChalleNGe's mission. Some sites also create awareness by advertising ChalleNGe on traditional or social media outlets. The aim of this outreach is to generate applicants who can be screened for eligibility and fit for ChalleNGe,[6] resulting in cadets admitted to the program. The final step in this phase is to get those students admitted to the program to actually show up and participate in acclimation.

Acclimation Phase

Activities in the acclimation phase are directed toward orienting new cadets to ChalleNGe. This includes conducting initial physical and placement tests, organizing teambuilding activities to instantiate a team mindset among cadets, and counseling cadets on program expectations, life skills, and well-being.

Residential Phase

The residential phase is where most program activities take place. These activities are generally organized around providing for cadets' basic needs (e.g., housing, sustenance, safety) and activities to develop the eight core components among cadets.

Outputs

ChalleNGe program outputs—the immediate products that result from program activities—include many of the metrics currently tracked by individual sites. For example, if program activities are accomplished, then cadets will be recruited to ChalleNGe, and they will engage in physical training, perform community service, etc., and eventually graduate and earn academic credentials or credits. The number and extent of these outcomes produced will hopefully meet the program site goals (e.g., the target number of graduates).

---

6 Screening generally includes an assessment of the applicant's background and an interview. While sites do not generally exclude applicants based on standardized test scores, sites do exclude applicants who have educational, physical, or psychological and emotional needs that cannot be met by the program. Age may also be considered, especially in cases when sites have more applicants than they can admit; sites may give preference to older cadets who could become ineligible due to age before the next cycle. There is no requirement that applicants meet military eligibility standards.

Outcomes

The changes in cadets that the ChalleNGe program is intended to produce are reflected in the logic model outcomes. These program outcomes can be assessed in the short, medium, and long terms. In the short term, if ChalleNGe produces outputs as intended, then graduates would be placed in school, the military, a job, or post-residential community service; earn a high school degree and/or a post-secondary credential; and have improved health, increased awareness and interest in military service, and improved life-coping skills. Those short-term outcomes would ideally translate into such medium-term outcomes as additional academic or professional credentials, better job skills, improved career opportunities and employment, and service to local communities and enhanced physical well-being. In the long term, ChalleNGe graduates would ideally exhibit characteristics of good citizenship: healthy social functioning and social interactions, participation in civic life, economic self-sufficiency, and physical well-being.

Note that the revised logic model is structured to show that short-, medium- and long-term outcomes at the individual graduate level all contribute to positive outcomes for communities and government, as well as the military. Ideally, ChalleNGe graduates would contribute to the workforce, support families, and contribute to a community's tax base and would not be contributing to crime or drug use rates as they might have without ChalleNGe. And to the extent that the public is aware of ChalleNGe, its influence on participating youth, and the graduate's positive life-course after the program, the program has the potential to enhance the public perception of the armed services. Finally, ChalleNGe staff often refer to their graduates as the best advertising for the ChalleNGe program, and graduates who successfully represent the ideal program outcomes will likely enhance the program's ability to recruit additional cadets from their home communities.

External Factors

The logic model also takes into account factors outside the program's direct control that can affect the program at all phases. For example, at the individual level, an unknown physical or mental health issue might affect cadets' ability to complete the program; at the family level, parents might not fully support keeping cadets in ChalleNGe when they want to leave, or graduates might return to a family or school environment that negatively affects their ability to gain employment or complete their education. At the community level, as state education departments introduce new programs to serve youth at risk of not completing high school, ChalleNGe sites may face increased competition for program recruiting. Similarly, the external labor market will affect a site's ability to hire and retain high-quality staff members or even influence post-residential placement of ChalleNGe graduates. State-level elections or turnover in National Guard leadership (e.g., the Adjutant General) may shift state-level support and subsequent resource availability for program sites. Changes in national-level policy (e.g., military recruitment tiers) also have the potential to influence program outputs and outcomes. While these conditions are not easily changed or modified by individual sites, the program sites must adapt to address these changing conditions to continually provide the best available services to their target population.

Outcomes That ChalleNGe Currently Reports

The ChalleNGe program currently reports on a small subset of short-term outcomes for its program graduates. Namely, the sites focus on the number and proportion of ChalleNGe graduates who have post-residential placements in any combination of school, workforce (nonmilitary), military, or community service. Sites collect data on program graduates, either through self-report or from the graduate's mentor, for each of the 12 months following program completion.[7] Sites are able to track changes over the post-residential phase (i.e., increases or decreases in placement rates from Month 3 to Month 6), as well as compare placement rates of the current graduates with those from prior ChalleNGe classes.

There are three key issues with these currently reported outcomes. First, these outcomes focus predominantly on only three out of the eight core components: academic excellence, service to community, and job skills. Sites do not currently measure short-term outcomes for the other five core components. Second, the current outcomes are relatively crude measures. For example, an educational placement includes graduates who returned to a traditional high school and those who enrolled in a postsecondary program. A job placement can include a part-time minimum-wage position as well as a full-time job that requires a credential, provides economic stability, and has the potential for long-term career growth. In addition to providing very little information about the characteristics of the placement, the current outcome measures do not capture an individual's progress. For example, the data do not provide the ability to detect when an individual completes high school, either with a regular diploma or a General Educational Development (GED) credential, and moves on to a postsecondary credentialing program during the post-residential phase. In both cases, these are reported as "educational placements," and yet that individual has made noticeable progress toward positive, long-term change.

The third issue is that the outcomes measured are the same regardless of site context or programmatic choices. Each site operates within a local context that shapes what that site can offer to cadets during the residential phase and, in turn, the potential placements of those cadets after program graduation. The variation across local contexts may help explain nuances in program trends and differences in outcomes over time and across program sites. In other words, comparing outcomes across the many ChalleNGe sites may not be an appropriate or fair comparison without consideration given to contextual differences. We present a deeper dive into contextual factors that are important to ChalleNGe program implementa-

[7] Mentors play a key role in reporting placement information. Not all graduates or mentors provide the expected monthly updates; nonreporting becomes more common as the months after graduation pass. The pilot program described in Appendix D provides some insights into the mentoring program and the difficulties inherent in collecting data through mentors.

tion across sites in Appendix A; this type of contextual awareness will assist in making sense of site and program outcomes measured now and in the future. Additionally, understanding these contextual differences may shape the type of outcomes that are used to assess program effectiveness for specific sites. For example, sites offering fully accredited high schools may be asked to report graduate completion of a regular high school diploma, while sites focusing on GED preparation may be asked to report what proportion of program graduates successfully attain a GED within the post-residential phase. Such an approach ties the outcome measures more directly to program resources and activities.

Conclusion

In this chapter, we reviewed the design of the ChalleNGe program and provided an updated version of the program logic model. The logic model provides guidance on how to think about ways that program resources and activities can generate measurable impacts on the lives of cadets and the greater community. We also compared the outcomes in the logic model with the data that sites typically collect. We identified some weaknesses in existing ChalleNGe outcome data: The measures collected do not typically cover all of the core components, the outcome measures lack nuance, and the measures are not contextualized.

Later in this report, we provide several suggestions that could be used to broaden the number of outcomes included and to sharpen the specific measures. We do not provide specific recommendations to contextualize the measures, but we do point out the need to consider context when reporting data. But before providing further detail on data and recommendations, we discuss program-level trends in the following chapter.

CHAPTER THREE

Program Trends

In this chapter, we use data gathered from the ChalleNGe sites to describe trends in a few key indicators throughout the period covered by this study. These data provide an overview of typical participation numbers, costs, and graduation rates; this information provides context for understanding the arena in which programs typically operate. Such trend analyses were possible only after collecting detailed, consistent data over the course of this project. This information also helps to establish a foundation for the discussion of program measurement in subsequent chapters.

Each of the four annual reports produced by RAND includes a brief trend analysis. The focus in these past reports has been on overall program trends—specifically the numbers of young people who applied to a ChalleNGe site, entered ChalleNGe, and completed ChalleNGe. Past reports also have noted graduation rates. Reports focusing on cadets from 2017 and earlier tracked the proportion of cadets who scored at or above the ninth-grade level on the Test of Adult Basic Education (TABE).[1] The total number of sites increased between 2015 and 2018 as sites opened, closed, merged, and suspended operations temporarily; given these changes, collecting and reporting consistent data has posed challenges.

Trends in Participants and Costs

Across the entire period covered by the last four annual reports (2015–2018), the ChalleNGe program showed modest increases in the numbers of applicants, entrants, and graduates; TABE scores were stable. However, the numbers of applicants, entrants, and graduates were somewhat lower in 2018 than in the previous three years (Constant et al., 2020). The decrease in 2018 appears to be linked to a modest decrease in the size of the largest programs.

Site-Level Participation

Here, we focus on site-level measures and trends, reporting consistent data for all sites that were operational during the course of the current project. A typical site has about 250 appli-

---

1 The newest version of the TABE was introduced and adopted by some sites in 2018; because these scores are not directly comparable with the scores on earlier versions, trend analyses after 2018 do not include overall TABE scores, although we do track the scores by test version.

cants per class; aside from an uptick in late 2016, this number has remained roughly constant over the 2015–2018 period (see Figure 3.1).[2] Over this period, a typical site had about 150 entrants in each class, of which about 120 cadets graduated from ChalleNGe at a typical site (about 80 percent). The average numbers of entrants and graduates decreased slightly over this period, but the changes have been small.[3] There are differences between sites, but the overall program graduation rate remained roughly constant between 2015 and 2018 at about 80 percent.[4]

FIGURE 3.1
Trends in Applicants, Entrants, and Graduates at ChalleNGe Sites, 2015–2018

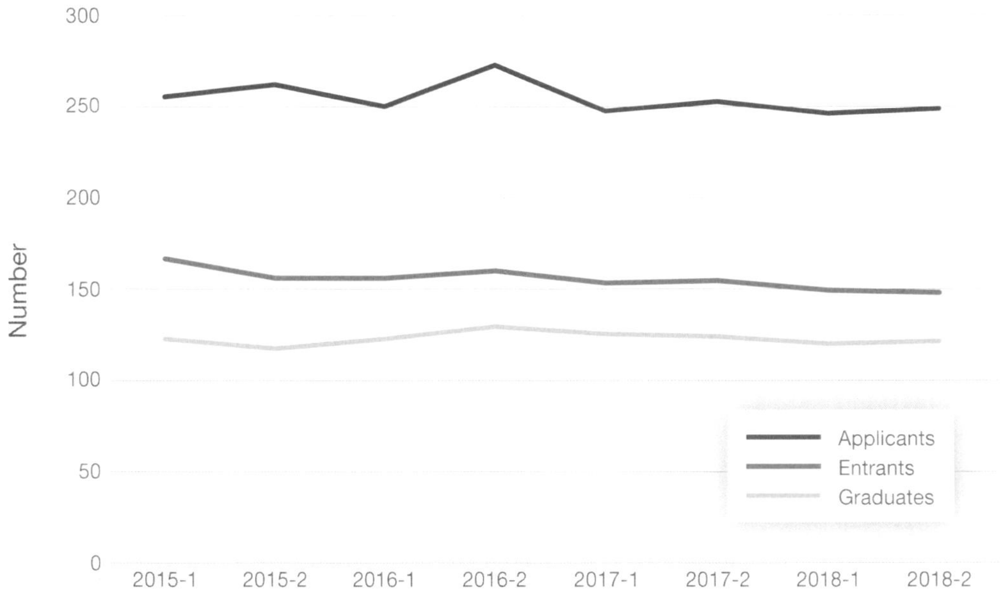

SOURCE: Authors' calculations using RAND annual data collection.
NOTE: -1 designates that year's January-start class, and -2 designates that year's July-start class.

---

2 The uptick in 2016 was not driven by a single site or a small group of sites.

3 The numbers reported in Figure 3.1 are means; median figures tend to be slightly smaller, but the trends are very similar. The number of sites did change over this period—new sites opened in California, Georgia, North Carolina, and Tennessee. The two Texas sites consolidated into a single site in 2018. By class 51 (in late 2018), there were four more sites than at the beginning of 2015.

4 The graduation rate calculation is sensitive to analytical decisions and to changes in the data included. In 2015, some sites reported slightly different numbers on the site-level worksheet than in the cadet-level data; in later years, program-level and cadet-level data match. Here, we use program-level data; using cadet-level data results in somewhat lower graduation rates for the 2015 classes. Also, graduation rates differ by site and by site characteristics. In future analyses, RAND researchers plan to focus on graduation rates among subpopulations.

Program Costs

Next, we present some descriptive analyses of program costs. For context, the 2015–2018 period was marked by relatively low inflation but also the continuation of an earlier trend in education—considerable upward cost pressures on postsecondary institutions. Over the past 20 years, the average annual cost of attending college has increased by 2 to 5 percent per year *after* adjusting for inflation.[5] Therefore, the inflation-adjusted cost of college (at a public two- or four-year institution) has increased by 50 to 100 percent since 2000. While state-run public postsecondary institutions face different cost pressures than the ChalleNGe program, ChalleNGe sites may compete with postsecondary institutions for instructors and other materials. Therefore, such cost pressures *may* have an influence on the ChalleNGe program.

Our past analyses showed that the average cost per cadet of the ChalleNGe program was roughly $20,000 in 2015 (Wenger et al., 2017). The average cost varied across sites: Smaller sites had higher costs, but per-cadet costs were similar at most sites reporting at least 150 graduates per year (recall that a typical site has about 240 graduates per year, or about 120 graduates per class).

Between 2015 and 2018, costs per cadet and costs per graduate increased. Figure 3.2 plots yearly costs per cadet and per graduate in 2019 dollars (thus, all costs are adjusted for inflation). Reported costs per participant and per graduate were flat in 2015–2016 and increased in 2017–2018.[6] 2018 costs were about 10 percent higher than 2015 costs (as shown by the solid green and solid blue lines).

The opening of new sites appears to explain much of this trend. New sites tend to be somewhat more expensive than well-established sites because new sites frequently have small numbers of participants. Per-site costs rose only slightly among established sites—the dotted green line indicates the inflation-adjusted cost per graduate when we include only sites that operated continuously throughout the 2015–2018 period. When including only continuously operating sites, we estimate that per-graduate costs have increased about 3 percent, while per-entrant costs have increased by roughly 5 percent (see the dotted blue line).

---

5 See College Board, 2019—but note that this citation uses published prices; students may pay lower prices after financial aid.

6 In 2016 and later years, we explicitly requested information on federal funds, state match, and other sources of revenue. We requested only federal and state funds in 2015. It is possible that some sites included other sources of funding in the 2015 data call; if this is the case, then the 2015 figure may represent a modest overstatement of the true costs that year. The Maryland site did not report funding data in 2016 (although the site reported other data). We estimated its 2016 funding using 2015 and 2017 information. Across the sites, we adjust for inflation by using the Consumer Price Index for urban consumers; see U.S. Bureau of Labor Statistics, 2020.

FIGURE 3.2
Average Cost per Participant at ChalleNGe Sites, 2015–2018

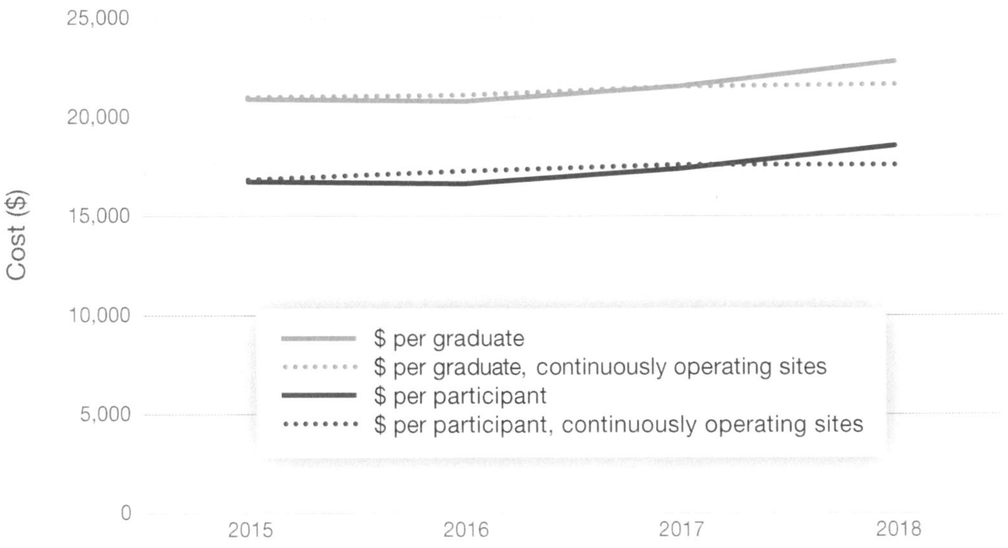

SOURCE: Authors' calculations using RAND annual data collection.
NOTE: Continuous costs (per graduate and per participant) are calculated by including only the sites that operated continuously during the 2015–2018 period.

Conclusion

During the 2015–2018 period, a typical site had about 150 entrants in each class, of which about 120 cadets graduated from ChalleNGe (about 80 percent). The average numbers of entrants and graduates decreased slightly over this period, and spending on ChalleNGe sites increased slightly. The increase in costs is far lower than increases in most postsecondary institutions, and much of the increase is related to opening new programs. Finally, the costs per participant and per graduate remain modest when compared with other youth programs (Wenger et al., 2017).

CHAPTER FOUR

Existing Data and Approaches to Program Measurement

In the previous chapters of this report, we described the design of the ChalleNGe program, presented a logic model of how ChalleNGe operates and brings about change in participants, and highlighted trends in several key indicators during the period covered by this study. We now shift our attention to address current approaches to data collection and outcome measurement. This discussion will provide a foundation for understanding how the program can better measure progress toward meeting its mission.

Progress measurement requires data collection to support assessment of the desired measures of program implementation and program effectiveness. That is to say, data are needed to measure core operations, outputs, and outcomes, as these measures can be used to assess the extent to which the program is producing the intended outcomes and identify areas of success and areas for improvement. Having these measures and focusing on key performance indicators also enables the program and individual sites to provide empirically grounded evidence of program success to potential recruits and their families, community organizations that support or partner with the program, key stakeholders, and the broader public.

We begin this chapter by broadly describing the requirements for data collection. We then describe current data collection at ChalleNGe sites in relation to the various components of the logic model presented in Chapter Two. As part of this discussion, we note some types of data that are *not* collected, but we neither assess the quality of the data (i.e., the proportion of missing, incorrect, or otherwise problematic data entries) nor prescribe specific alternatives to the current data. Such analysis is beyond the focus of this report. (Note that in Chapter Five, we describe broad approaches to collecting data on long-term outcomes, and we provide recommendations for areas of focus within the large long-term outcomes measures). But in this chapter, we do include a discussion of challenges that need to be addressed to expand data collection, especially for long-term outcomes. Finally, we briefly discuss some other resources that might be leveraged to guide future data collection.

Data Requirements

The goal of any data collection effort is to minimize the burden of the data collection while simultaneously maximizing the benefit of what can be learned from those data. The types of information collected, as well as the format or structure of that information, should be driven by the purpose the data will serve (Yoo, Whitaker, and McCombs, 2019). For example, ChalleNGe stakeholders may need to understand staff turnover each year. If stakeholders want only an overall rate of turnover, collecting aggregate counts of the number of total staff each class cycle and the number of new staff in each class cycle would likely be sufficient to address the need. If, however, stakeholders desire to improve staffing policies to reduce turnover, then data about the individual staff members (e.g., years working at ChalleNGe, years of military service, education level, assigned shift and role) may be needed, along with the date of position entry, date of position exit, and the reason the staff member departed the position. These person-level data enable analyses to understand, for example, any patterns in turnover: Staff may tend to turn over after a set period of time, or the most inexperienced staff may be the most likely to leave, or staff who work the third shift may leave at high rates. These different types of turnover would likely have different causes and would suggest different responses. Therefore, the types of data collected determine what can be learned from the data, and a review of the data needs of ChalleNGe programs should guide any modification or expansion of data collection efforts in the short and longer terms.

Data Currently Collected by ChalleNGe Sites

We now discuss data currently collected by ChalleNGe sites. We first examine the data that sites provide for annual performance calculations.[1] Once a year over the past four years, the RAND research team has requested data from each site; each *data call* includes aggregate information on the number of participants and staff members, basic funding information, and information on each site's activities and offerings. These data calls also include deidentified information describing individual cadets' test scores and placement information during the 12 months postgraduation.

Beyond these data calls, sites collect other information—staff discussed some aspects of these data during site visits. Thus, to better understand all the existing data and identify data gaps, in 2019 we developed and fielded a brief data questionnaire, which we distributed to all 39 ChalleNGe sites that were operational at that time. We present the results of this questionnaire below.

[1] We recognize that individual sites may collect additional data beyond what is required, and that may serve a specific purpose or goal for those sites. However, these additional data should supplement a robust but streamlined and common data collection and management system that would reduce burden on programs and ensure consistent findings and recommendations for all entities that work with ChalleNGe data.

We tie the data components, where feasible, to the ChalleNGe logic model to show what aspects of the program are currently measured. This data review is a critical first step in the process of identifying gaps in current data, data needs for the future, and general ways to enhance data collection across the ChalleNGe sites.

Inputs

As part of each data call, RAND researchers request data in aggregate form on the number of staff members in each role (e.g., cadre, administrative, counseling), the number of new staff in each role over the last 12-month period, the number of staff who work full time in each position, and the entry-level salary for each role. Each ChalleNGe site also provides information on its annual funding, including the dollar amount of both federal and state funds provided for the program. Sites also outline other streams of financial support and the source of those funds, including in-kind donations. For example, some sites have previously secured one-time grants for facility maintenance or expanding programmatic offerings, while other sites have foundations to provide assistance to the program when cadets have basic needs that the programs are not able to fund (e.g., broken eyeglasses, running shoes). The funding data provided for the calculation of annual per cadet expenditures, when combined with other data about the site (e.g., years of operation), can provide insights into the cost differentials of long-run programs as compared with a program that was recently stood up.

Sites relayed some information about mentors during our site visits, but those data have not been gathered systematically across the sites. Per the data inventory, all sites collect at least some basic information on the mentors they partner with to support cadets during and after the residential phase. These data, which more than 70 percent of programs maintain electronically, include the mentor's home ZIP code, age, occupation, and how long the mentor has known the cadet. Many sites collect these data during the application period, while other sites gather the data again or for the first time during pre-ChalleNGe or the ChalleNGe residential phase.

While the sites have background data on mentors, no information is systematically collected on the quality of mentor-mentee relationships or the reason(s) that meetings between mentors and mentees cease to occur. Collecting and analyzing information about mentors and their mentor-mentee experiences might provide insights into which types of mentors are more successful than others at forming relationships with cadets and why some mentor-mentee relationships falter. Although such information collection could require substantial resources, it could also indicate specific policy changes that might increase program effectiveness.[2]

While RAND researchers have collected data on the financial and human assets of ChalleNGe sites for progress and performance measurement, our data collection has not focused on the policy, guidance documents, or planning resources that structure how sites set up

---

2 We discuss the results from a short pilot program to improve mentor training in Appendix D.

and implement the program. Some of these relationships are governed by publicly available documents or agreements; examples include agreements between specific sites and their local partners or between specific sites and the National Guard Bureau.

Activities

The ChalleNGe logic model separates activities into three phases: recruitment and application, acclimation, and residential. These phases may be enacted concurrently for different ChalleNGe classes. For example, staff at a site actively recruit for the next class cycle while implementing the residential phase for the current ChalleNGe class. Each phase is critical for programs to successfully implement the full program each year.

Recruitment and Application Phase

Each ChalleNGe site seeks a target number of recruits to start and finish each ChalleNGe class. Directors are often able to provide an immediate response to the question of how many applications they need to reach their graduation target for a class. Sites provide, at minimum, an aggregate count of applicants for each class as part of RAND's annual data request. Some programs provide person-level information about applicants, including demographic information (e.g., age, gender) that is collected and stored in the site's cadet data system.[3] The aggregate count of applicants provides an annual trend of recruitment. Each site also provides an aggregate count, per class, of individuals who enter pre-ChalleNGe. The cadet data system files, for most sites, also include indicators of whether an applicant was admitted to the program and whether the applicant entered pre-ChalleNGe. These data are essential to the recruitment phase and can help programs understand recruitment trends and challenges over time. Starting in 2019, the annual data call also requested program-level information about recruitment strategies, including the use of social media and relationship development with counseling, education, and juvenile justice professionals.

The data inventory highlights the fact that many programs collect information beyond basic demographics (e.g., age, gender) about applicants and maintain these data in electronic formats. For example, all sites collect age, race, gender, and home ZIP code. All but one site collects Social Security number at the application phase, more than 90 percent of sites track the school of last enrollment, and approximately two-thirds of the ChalleNGe sites ask for height and weight on the application. Having these data for all sites could enable additional analyses to determine the extent to which applicants reflect the state demographic profile or help identify recruitment regions that are either over- or underrepresented to inform future recruitment efforts. Finally, almost 90 percent of programs also track why each individual sought to participate in ChalleNGe; these data could help recruiters understand where ChalleNGe has potential recruitment advantages over competing alternative education programs.

---

3 The term *cadet data system* is used to broadly capture the data systems, such as Cadet Tracker or other site-specific electronic systems, used to store and track cadet data.

Acclimation Phase

The *acclimation*, or *pre-ChalleNGe*, phase is the period when new recruits show up to the site and begin their adjustment to life at ChalleNGe. In addition to team building and providing participants with an introduction to drill and physical training, ChalleNGe sites frequently use the acclimation phase to administer assessments in preparation for ChalleNGe. As mentioned above, sites provide a count of the number of candidates that begin pre-ChalleNGe for each class. They also provide a count of the number of candidates who successfully enter ChalleNGe (i.e., they complete the pre-ChalleNGe phase). For the sites that include applicant and candidate data in the cadet data system files, current analyses can expand to identify differences in the individuals who do or do not persist to ChalleNGe.[4]

Residential Phase

The *residential phase* is the 22-week period during which cadets' basic needs are provided for as they receive the eight core components of ChalleNGe. Each site identifies the focus of the academic instruction that cadets receive at the program, with the option to select multiple responses when the site offers multiple pathways. These pathways include offering completion of a high school diploma, credit recovery, or GED-focused instruction. Data specific to the residential phase are limited, mostly because the results of these activities are predominantly measured as outputs and will be discussed in the next section. However, site artifacts of the residential phase can provide insights into the implementation of the program. A site's program calendar, combined with its staff and cadet daily schedules, provides data for calculating the amount of daily physical exercise or academic instruction that cadets receive, the amount of in-person interaction a cadet has with the mentor during the residential period, or even how much downtime a cadet is given each day. The schedules also show how the sites structure community service or enrichment activities during the weekend and over weekends, as well as how sites time their home pass(es) and family days. The site's Post-Residential Action Plan document also provides insight into what conversations staff have to prepare cadets for post-residential life.

Outputs

The annual data call has sought a substantive amount of information on cadet outputs. The outputs are the crux of what cadets receive from participating in the program. In many cases, positive outputs are the result of the program being implemented as intended. As shown in Figure 2.1, many of the program outputs relate to the eight core components of ChalleNGe, with a few additional aspects of program implementation also considered outputs. As discussed in the activities section, data are available for which cadets are recruited and success-

[4] California Discovery, Florida, Maryland, and South Carolina provide data on graduates only. It is likely that these sites track information on applicants, arrivals, candidates, and cadets who do not complete the program even if the sites do not currently share this data.

fully start the full residential phase of ChalleNGe. During the residential phase, the following data are collected regarding program participation and the core components of ChalleNGe:

- *Physical fitness* is measured through changes in the number of pushups and the time it takes to run one mile.
- *Academic excellence* is measured through changes in TABE assessment scores, as well as through successful completion of a high school diploma or a high school equivalency test.
- *Service to community* is measured as an average number of hours completed by program graduates.
- *Responsible citizenship* is measured by the proportion of cadets eligible to vote who are registered to vote and the proportion of eligible cadets who have registered for Selective Service. These numbers are provided in aggregate form by each site and are not yet measured at the cadet level.

Each site also provides data on the average number of career and technical education (CTE) or vocational credits, as well as college credits that cadets earn while in the residential phase. These data are provided at the site level and for each individual cadet. And finally, in the cadet data system files, each site provides an indicator for which cadets successfully complete the residential phase and graduate from ChalleNGe. The data on program graduates are used to track the overall trends in ChalleNGe graduates over time and by site. These data are also used to identify whether each site has met its target number of graduates for the class cycle.

The data questionnaire administered to sites suggests opportunities to expand on the measurement of the eight core components and to create indicators of cadet outputs on other not-yet-measured aspects of the logic model. For example, most sites report keeping electronic records of cadet performance related to job skills instruction (90 percent), life skills instruction (90 percent), health and hygiene (87 percent), and leadership/followership (90 percent), which would potentially enable reporting on all eight core components of ChalleNGe. All sites track information about cadet disciplinary infractions, most of which are also tracked in the cadet data system. Additionally, all sites track both the date a cadet exits ChalleNGe, if the cadet does not persist to graduation, and the reason for the early exit. Each of these data points, if measured in similar ways across sites, expands on what we know about each site and, more broadly, the program. Most notably, sites suggest that there are data available such that all eight core components of the ChalleNGe program model can be measured and integrated into annual reporting. Sites can use this expanded reporting not only to review their own data but also to examine trends relative to other sites. These additional insights may help identify program successes or highlight best practices that can be leveraged across sites to improve program operations.

Outcomes

The changes in cadets resulting from their participation in ChalleNGe are identified as the short-, medium-, and long-term outcomes. In this section, we focus on the short-term outcomes of the ChalleNGe logic model. ChalleNGe sites are required to report on the short-term outcomes of graduate placement into school, the military, the labor market, and/or a community service organization. To our knowledge, sites do not systematically collect data on medium- and long-term outcomes of their program graduates.[5]

The data questionnaire illuminates additional outcome-related data that programs collect,[6] and these data go beyond whether a cadet has a post-residential placement. All sites report tracking whether those who report employment are working full time or part time, and 37 of the sites report collecting employer information (e.g., company name, location) and the number of hours worked in an average week. Seventy-two percent of programs (i.e., 28 sites) also collect information on the wages of their graduates during the post-residential phase. We found similar detailed data collections related to educational attainment. All sites report collecting data on the type of educational institution graduates are placed in (e.g., high school, technical school). Many sites also collect information on high school graduation (30 sites), as well as high school equivalency attainment (32 sites) and progress (29 sites) that occurs during the post-residential period. For graduates joining the military, all sites collect the date service is set to begin, and, except for one site, all collect data on the type of enlistment (e.g., active duty, guard) and the service branch. Finally, two-thirds of sites collect information on the living arrangements (e.g., living with parents, grandparents, alone) of graduates. Collectively, these expanded data during the post-residential phase have the potential to increase our knowledge about the extent to which participation in ChalleNGe leads to intended outcomes and how those outcomes are or are not realized differently with varying cadet background and ChalleNGe-provided experiences.

Current Data Gaps

Figure 4.1 provides a visual representation of the current status of ChalleNGe data. The components for which there are data currently used for progress and performance monitoring are represented in green text; the components for which some sites report having data that may be leveraged in the future are represented in orange text; and those components for which no or limited sites report data are represented in purple text. Gray and black text reflects aspects of the model that we did not investigate for the purpose of this report.

---

5 In Appendix E of this report, we discuss a survey administered to the graduates of WYA as the site celebrated its tenth anniversary; the survey included longer-term outcomes.

6 Sites were asked, in the data inventory, the extent to which they collect outcome-related data beyond the 12 months of the post-residential period. No more than four sites reported collecting any single indicator (e.g., employment, wages, high school or GED completion) of graduate outcomes.

FIGURE 4.1
ChalleNGe Logic Model, with the Current Status of Data Availabilities

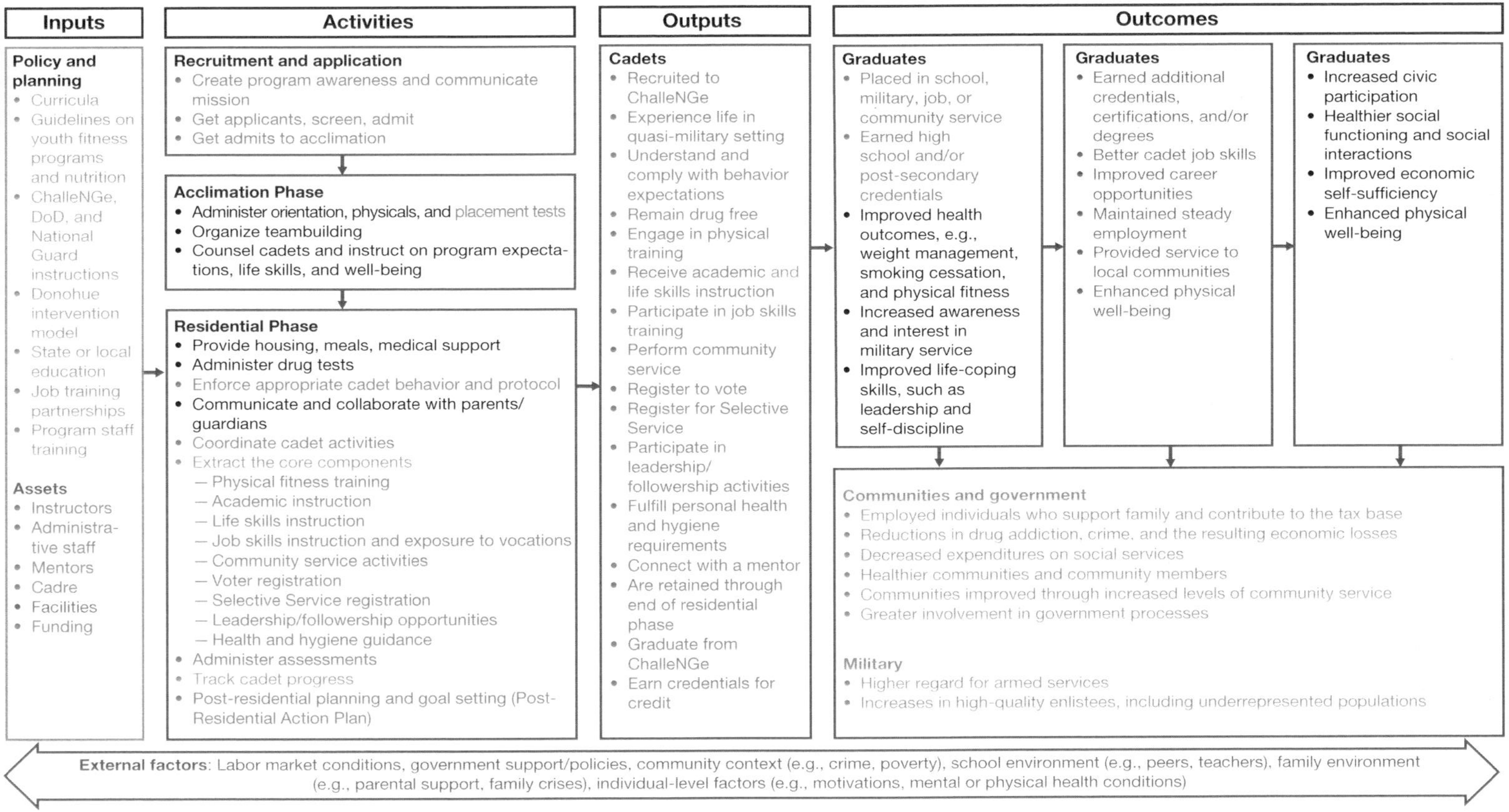

NOTES: Green text reflects components for which data are currently available and used for progress and performance monitoring; orange text reflects components for which some sites report having data that could be leveraged in the future; purple text reflects those components for which no or limited sites have reported data; gray and black text reflects aspects of the model that we did not investigate for the purpose of this report.

As can be seen in Figure 4.1, the largest gap in data collection is related to short-, medium-, and long-term outcomes of program graduates. This is not surprising, since collecting these data has not been required. However, given the interest in expanding data collection to additional years of the post-residential phase, this gap suggests that there is substantial work to be done in this area.

While there is increased interest in expanding the collection and measurement of graduate outcomes, ChalleNGe should also continue to identify key inputs, activities, and outputs for which there are limited or no data. These aspects of program implementation are especially important to assess for such programs as ChalleNGe that have medium- or long-term outcomes that are not being measured or for which outcome measurement is difficult. The rationale for focusing on the implementation side of the logic model is that, if the program is not operating as intended, there is a lower likelihood that the desired outcomes are being produced by the program. Thus, improving program implementation and operations should help bring about the desired outcomes.

Another key issue is data quality, which can be influenced by several factors, including the instruments and methods used to collect data, data entry methods, and the data management system. Tools that incorporate consistency and error checks at all stages of data collection and management are likely to highlight problems that can be corrected. Moreover, collected data that are used consistently and regularly are likely to be subject to more regular checks that help identify and address data problems early.

Another type of data that might be collected involves measures of quality. Ultimately, such data could be critical to enhancing program implementation and outcomes. These types of data might include the quality of inputs and resources, the extent to which activities incorporate best practices, and the depth of engagement that cadets have with the core components of the program. Measures of data quality can provide more insights than simple measures, such as class attendance and community service hours completed. For example, measures of quality might include the pedagogical approaches that are used in the classroom to engage cadets, the types of community service activities cadets engage in, and self-reported experiences with those activities. Collecting information that captures the quality of relevant inputs, activities, and outputs can help identify opportunities to improve program operations. This is especially important for programs such as ChalleNGe that face difficulty capturing longer-term indicators.

ChalleNGe leadership and site directors will need to think critically about implementing any changes to current practices, given that the sites do not use a single, shared administrative data system. Implementing new or changed data collection practices will require intentional and targeted support to ensure that the selected data collection practices can be implemented in appropriate ways across the many ChalleNGe sites to address various data system limitations or requirements while simultaneously maintaining data consistency and quality for the program. This is true of data related to inputs, activities, and outputs and applies also to collecting information on the outcomes for program graduates.

Challenges to Address Before Expanding or Modifying Current Data Collection

As part of the data inventory, we asked sites to identify any difficulties that they have related to collecting and maintaining data, as well as the conditions that sites need to have met to address the recent emphasis on tracking program graduates for up to five years after the end of the residential phase.[7] Nine sites (23 percent) reported that they do not face any difficulties in collecting or maintaining data. Twenty-three sites identified at least one of the following issues as a challenge:

- insufficient training for using Cadet Tracker (15 sites)
- lack of documented materials on how to enter and maintain data (13 sites)
- lack of dedicated time and staffing (13 sites)
- lack of sufficient resources (e.g., equipment, internet bandwidth) (9 sites)
- incorrect data reported from other ChalleNGe departments (6 sites).

A total of 18 sites identified that they faced additional challenges, only seven of which specified a challenge other than the supplied response options. The most common of these additional challenges were predominantly of two types and reported by nine and eight sites, respectively. First, Cadet Tracker is problematic in that the system can crash with some frequency; repairing or updating the system takes time and is difficult, especially on military installations or in remote locations; and, for those sites looking to follow performance trends during and between class cycles, the system has limited functionality for reporting and does not enhance data utilization or internal evaluation capabilities. The second major challenge that sites reported is loss of or difficulty in maintaining sufficient contact with mentors and graduates to collect 12 months of placement data during the post-residential phase. Both of these challenges have implications for the program's ability to meet its goal of collecting additional years of outcome data for graduates.

The data tracking system was also the most-chosen enhancement that sites need in order to address the recent emphasis on collecting long-term issues. Twenty-seven sites identified the need for a ChalleNGe-wide centralized data system that enables centralized collection and management of outcomes, including GED, high school diploma attainment, and employment and military enlistment. The other two needs most commonly identified by sites are (1) clear guidance on exactly what is expected to be collected (26 sites) and (2) resources to hire new dedicated staff and build new infrastructure to meet this reporting need (24 sites). These responses suggest that sites lack the infrastructure, human capital, and guidance that they need to forge ahead in collecting longer-term outcome data on their program graduates.

---

[7] Sites were instructed to select all difficulties that applied from a preconstructed list and were provided an option of a write-in response.

Other Resources That Might Be Leveraged to Guide Future Data Collection

Setting aside the issues of current capacity to handle new or modified data collection, we want to provide some insight that may be helpful for ChalleNGe to consider when identifying additional data and performance measures in the future. After conducting a review of the current data collected and the quality of those data, we considered how data are used by programs that serve similar populations; employ similar or aligned approaches to improving the lives of at-risk youth; or target similar short-, medium-, and longer-term outcomes. We reviewed the approaches to data collection and the types of data collected by Workforce and Innovation Opportunity Act programs for youth, including YouthBuild, Reentry Employment Opportunities, and Youth Program; Job Corps; and nonfederal programs targeted for at-risk youth, including the Marion Barry Youth Summer Employment Program (MBYSEP) and Check and Connect. We describe each of these programs and their affiliated data in Appendix B. Given the job and career focus of these programs, it is not surprising that the measures in Appendix B are designed to document progress in training and employment. However, the ChalleNGe model has a much broader focus and aims to influence many other outcomes (again, see Figure 4.1). Therefore, the RAND team also reviewed existing measures that focus on other key components, such as citizenship, leadership/followership, and service to community; we document these measures in Appendix C. While it may not be feasible for ChalleNGe to perfectly replicate these data approaches, the program can benefit from understanding what similar programs use and how ChalleNGe data and evaluation practices compare.

Conclusion

All data collection activities should be conducted with purpose. This chapter focused on reviewing current systematic ChalleNGe data collections; identifying additional areas in which program monitoring and measurement may be feasible in the near future, given the data maintained by sites; and illuminating current gaps in program-related data. ChalleNGe must be intentional in its pathway forward, addressing both the infrastructure and the processes needed to collect data across all its sites and to ensure that the data being collected will provide the insights necessary to guide future decisionmaking about program operations.

CHAPTER FIVE

Approaches for Measuring Long-Term Outcomes and Determining Program Effectiveness

The mission of ChalleNGe is to "intervene in and reclaim" young peoples' lives (National Guard Youth ChalleNGe, undated). Thus, the ability to track cadets' progress and success long after they graduate from the program is critical. Indeed, determining how well ChalleNGe sites are doing at meeting their mission requires all sites to measure cadets' long-term outcomes. That said, sites have considerable flexibility in *how* they choose to meet this requirement.

In this chapter, we describe several broad approaches to tracking longer-term outcomes. Some ChalleNGe sites have already begun to put strategies in place to measure outcomes or are experimenting with other efforts that may make outcome measurement easier. As we discuss the broad strategies, we provide additional information about specific sites' relevant efforts, which can serve as examples to sites that are looking for ways to improve their ability to collect data on graduate long-term outcomes.

Next, we lay out a general and flexible framework for determining what types of information to collect, how frequently to collect the information, and how to interpret and analyze the information. Finally, we discuss lessons learned and implications for the sites and the program.

Approaches for Long-Term Tracking

In general, approaches for tracking long-term outcomes can be categorized as follows:

- **Maintain** contact with each graduate (or with a random subsample of graduates).
- Periodically **survey** graduates.
- **Match** graduates to information in existing state- or national-level databases.

There is some potential overlap between the approaches; for example, surveys could be used as part of a strategy to maintain contact with graduates. But, in general, maintaining contact involves continuing to communicate with each graduate (or with a sample of graduates) on a regular basis after the end of the 17.5-month ChalleNGe program. Periodically surveying graduates means developing and fielding short surveys on a regular schedule. Matching graduate information generally implies accessing one of the available state- or national-level databases and matching graduates' identifying information. For some—or perhaps many—sites, a combination of the approaches listed above might be most appropriate.

Maintain Contact with Each Graduate

Maintaining contact with each graduate can be thought of as extending the post-residential window of ChalleNGe beyond 12 months. Currently, mentors play a key role in supporting cadets as they transition from ChalleNGe to their next steps and play a key role in collecting information on cadets' placements. During ChalleNGe's 12-month post-residential period, mentors and mentees are expected to meet regularly, and mentors are expected to provide reports on mentee placement. However, mentor reporting falls off sharply during the year. For example, in 2017, sites reported that 25 to 30 percent of mentors were no longer providing reports by Month 6 (Wenger, Constant, and Cottrell, 2018).

RAND researchers worked with program staff at one ChalleNGe site to provide additional mentor training (see Appendix D). Mentors responded positively to the training, but those mentors who answered a follow-up survey three months after graduation indicated that they had far lower levels of interaction with cadets than the program recommends (again, see Appendix D). Further training could serve to improve mentor-mentee relationships and perhaps could increase the level of mentor reporting, but, given the challenges inherent in this system, long-term tracking is likely to involve *transitioning to a system in which sites collect information directly from graduates.* Sites in California and West Virginia have begun to experiment with longer-term tracking of graduates.

California efforts have focused on developing a tailored database. The Discovery program in California plans to track graduates for five years; case managers have the responsibility to contact graduates with an online survey every six months. This process is augmented with information gathered from social media accounts, as well as with phone calls to cadets, parents, and mentors. The program has collected information on about 40 percent of graduates through these means so far. Discovery employs three case managers and a support specialist, who are responsible for following up with 100–120 graduates each. The intent is to analyze the information that they are currently collecting in a systematic manner, with a focus on program improvements and providing information on program successes. The site's model includes initial resources for development of a custom database, willingness to work with an external organization, and a plan to use external expertise for training of staff and for system maintenance. While the total cost of this effort is not yet clear, this model does require substantial initial resources to develop the database, as well as ongoing resources for training and maintenance and to allow staff time to collect the information.

Mountaineer ChalleNGe Academy in West Virginia has taken a different approach: The site created a position to focus on tracking (*Graduate Specialist*) and hired a staff member in

July 2019.[1] The goal is to track all graduates for a five-year period after they leave the program. As of April 2020, the staff member had made progress in locating some of the graduates from the 2014–2015 period and was also working to maintain contact with more-recent graduates. The Graduate Specialist is using multiple methods—phone, email, and social media—to contact former cadets. This position is still relatively new; it is not yet possible to understand how many graduates can be located through these methods.

There are many ways for sites to maintain contact with graduates. Sites need not contact graduates every month, but touching base with graduates fairly frequently will facilitate efforts to collect data (e.g., sites may wish to experiment with collecting information every second month versus every quarter). Sites can use telephone calls, texts, or emails to prompt responses or could use a specialized app that allows graduates to report information. Sites might also develop and field short online surveys to collect information. Some methods may be more effective for some sites than others, and the best option for a site will likely depend on class size, staffing capacity and skills, and the methods by which the site currently organizes and stores placement information. Regardless of the particulars, collecting information on a regular basis over a long period of time means *establishing and nurturing a relationship with all graduates*.[2] There is already substantial variation in sites' approaches to collecting information; as discussed above, some sites are already experimenting with processes to collect longer-term, detailed information on all graduates. Experience gleaned by these sites will likely be of substantial benefit to other sites as well.

Sites with large numbers of graduates could consider selecting a random sample of graduates and focusing on collecting information only from the sample. This approach has an obvious advantage—collecting information from fewer graduates will require fewer resources. However, to ensure that the results are representative of all graduates, the site must select the sample in a random fashion and must maintain contact with all or nearly all of the graduates in this sample.[3]

Sites that undertake this type of data collection should focus on collecting multiple types of contact information before graduates leave ChalleNGe (and all sites will likely benefit from collecting multiple types of information). For example, sites may wish to collect cell phone numbers, mailing addresses, email addresses, and social media account information of cadets and some subset of this information on three close contacts (e.g., grandparents, friends, adult

---

1 This position includes other responsibilities, such as handling the program's social media and teaching an elective.

2 See Pollard and Baird, 2017, for a description of a panel survey that has effectively maintained contact with participants and, thus, maintained a very high response rate over a long period of time. ChalleNGe graduates will likely be more mobile than the population as a whole as they obtain education and additional labor market experience; for this reason, maintaining regular contact with graduates will likely require substantial effort but should pay substantial dividends.

3 If the site cannot maintain contact with most or all graduates, weighting the results provides an option that has the potential to produce representative results. See the discussion on the next page related to surveying graduates.

siblings). Establishing LinkedIn accounts for cadets and encouraging cadets to join a Facebook group or to follow the site on Twitter may also provide avenues for data collection. Sites may also wish to publicize the idea of data collection with cadets and parents—if cadets and parents understand how the sites will use the data, this may help increase responsiveness. Finally, sites could provide cell phones to cadets; in some cases, paying for cell phone service could be a cost-effective way to collect this information (a pilot project to test such a strategy would be an appropriate first step).

Regardless of exactly how sites choose to maintain contact with former cadets, periodic, targeted *nudges* (reminders that are generally delivered through electronic means) have been shown to influence behavior and may be useful in maintaining contact with cadets (Thaler and Sunstein, 2008; Doss et al., 2019). As an example, programs could send messages to former cadets, including helpful information as well as reminders to update contact information or to provide information about current activities.

This section has described several options for maintaining contact with cadets. Note, however, that we do not assume that mentors will be the ones carrying out long-term data collection, and indeed we do not believe that mentors can or should play a central role in collecting information on cadets' longer-term outcomes. Appendix D discusses a pilot project to improve training provided to mentors; in the course of completing the pilot project and collecting feedback from mentors, we found that it was difficult to contact mentors and persuade them to complete a survey. Among the small proportion of mentors who completed the survey, many reported substantial barriers to remaining in contact with their mentees.

Periodically Survey Graduates

Periodic surveys of graduates provide a different approach to collecting information on long-term outcomes. Several aspects of surveys are attractive—for example, developing and fielding surveys using online platforms requires relatively little staff effort, and filling out a survey could require less time and effort of graduates than responding to phone calls or emails. Surveys also are quite flexible; changing the questions is straightforward, and it is possible to collect rich information about a variety of outcomes. The main drawback with surveys is that the sample may be unrepresentative—even with widespread advertising, survey take-up rates are low (Cook, Heath, and Thompson, 2000; Keeter et al., 2017), and those who choose to respond to a survey may differ systematically from those who choose not to respond.

Lessons from a pilot project provide insights into how a ChalleNGe survey might work for other sites. WYA, with input from RAND researchers, piloted an alumni survey. The response rate was low; somewhat less than 20 percent of all graduates completed the survey. And the responses may not represent the typical experience—although such characteristics as access to technology and free time could affect the decision to complete a survey, presumably the graduates who had the most positive experience will also be more willing than others to complete the survey (although it could also be the case that some alumni who are particularly in need of support are likely to remain in close contact with WYA). In any case, determining the extent to which a survey is representative is not straightforward. While the technique of survey weighting can be helpful in this situation, certain caveats remain. Weighting can produce a sample that is representative of the population, based on measurable characteristics (such as age, gender, ethnicity, test scores, year of entry, etc.). The weighted sample may still not be representative in terms of unmeasured characteristics—such as motivation or the extent to which the participant had a positive experience. Therefore, caveats generally will be necessary when working with and reporting information collected through a survey.[4]

Alumni who responded to the WYA survey had very positive outcomes in terms of educational attainment and labor force participation. Indeed, results indicate that about 85 percent of alumni had completed or would soon complete high school (by earning a traditional high school diploma). The predicted high school completion rate is even higher among the most recent classes (see Appendix E for more details about the information collected on the survey and the analytic techniques).

While deploying the survey required only minimal staff effort, matching respondents to administrative files proved to be considerably more difficult. Matching data requires both resources and technical rigor; this task would be very difficult for a typical ChalleNGe site to carry out during day-to-day program duties. One option is for future surveys to include a few individual characteristics that alumni can complete quickly (such as gender, age, and possibly the cadet platoon to which they belonged). This would allow the construction of weights without matching the survey to the administrative files. However, being able to match all the survey responses to the administrative files would allow for richer analyses and, perhaps, more-effective weighting. For example, a matched sample would provide insights into the effects of TABE scores, as well as measures of classroom performance and experience in leadership positions, on long-term outcomes. This type of matching could be done using the survey participant's name, if program staff have the analytic capacity and data available to do so.[5] A broader solution would be to create and maintain a single, program-wide administrative database, together with standard tools and templates to be used across sites. We discuss these options in more detail in the final chapter.

Match Graduates' Information to Existing Database(s)

Matching graduates' information to existing databases provides a different approach to collecting long-term outcomes. In this case, the site provides an outside entity with information on cadets, including critical personal identifiers (e.g., name, birthdate, Social Security number, state and ZIP code of last known residence); that entity matches and extracts the

4 Weighting requires information about the entire population—in this case, the population is made up of all graduates from the site. We designed weights using information from the site's administrative files (see Appendix E for more information on weighting).

5 Alternatively, many survey respondents could likely be matched to administrative files based on a combination of information: home ZIP code at entry, platoon, gender, month and year, etc. Future efforts should experiment to determine the minimal amount of information required for a reasonably accurate match.

relevant information for each individual. The National Student Clearinghouse is one example of such a database that contains information on student enrollment and course completion at the majority of U.S. postsecondary institutions.[6] Many states maintain multiple databases; these may include information on unemployment compensation, criminal justice outcomes, educational attainment, death records, and other measures. In some cases, working with these databases may require the development of specific data-sharing agreements. Another possibility would be to submit data to the Defense Manpower Data Center to determine enlistment rates and other aspects of military performance, although there would be a substantial administrative cost involved.

In every case, such matching would require technical rigor and resources. We recognize that individual sites are *not* well-equipped to carry out such analyses. Carrying out matches centrally (using data from all sites) would likely lead to efficiency gains in cases involving national databases.

Recommended Outcomes to Measure

The central principle behind our guidance on measuring long-term outcomes is that the resulting measures should allow staff and others to determine how well the program is doing in meeting its long-term mission. To this end, there are several types of measures that all sites should collect, but sites should also retain flexibility in collecting additional information based on the specific emphasis at a site or on staff understanding of cadets' strengths and weaknesses. We recommend that all sites collect, at a minimum, detailed information on educational attainment; labor force participation, including military service; and aspects of the other six core components of ChalleNGe. Sites also may wish to collect more than the minimum measures we recommend to gain a more complete understanding of whether the program is meeting its mission and to better relay the program's strengths.

Here, we offer one other consideration that will be relevant regardless of the specific types of measures that sites choose to collect. Program staff should be mindful of the potential ethical issues involved with collecting information on past participants, some of whom may still be minors. These issues may be more relevant to some types of data collection than others, but program staff should approach these issues with thought and planning.

Educational Attainment Data

We recommend that the program collect data on the educational attainment of its graduates. Young workers receive a substantial payoff from additional education, and those who complete high school are much more likely than those who do not to attend postsecondary institu-

[6] With proof of appropriate permissions, the National Student Clearinghouse will accept and match personal identifiers; this fee-based service has the capacity to reveal levels of postsecondary enrollment and completion among graduates.

tions. Collecting information about **high school completion** will allow those sites that award high school credits to determine an important aspect of program effectiveness; if ChalleNGe graduates struggle to complete high school after the residential phase, sites should seek to understand the reason(s) behind these struggles. Sites also should collect information about **GED completion** (if relevant), and all sites should collect information about **postsecondary enrollment and credits earned**, as well as information on any **participation in or completion of formal job training programs.** In some states, programs may be able to access this information from a central state educational database; in other states, programs may need to contact individual districts, schools, etc.

Data on Labor Force Participation and Military Service

We recommend collecting labor force–related data, which include, at a minimum, several measures based on the graduate's current job: **hourly earnings, hours worked per week, time at current job** (this could be collected by asking whether the respondent has begun a new job since the previous data collection), and **existence of benefits.** Another option would be to collect earnings data on a quarterly basis; this information could be easily compared with statistics collected by other national training programs. To develop a more complete picture of household finances, sites could ask about total household earnings or assets, as well as sources of public assistance.

Industry and **occupation** (which could be collected at an aggregated level, rather than collecting exact job titles) will prove helpful to sites for several reasons—these measures will provide information about jobs available and thus may be helpful in considering types of CTE or similar training to offer to current or future ChalleNGe cadets. To be clear, some alumni may work in industries or occupations well beyond the training they completed, and this is not a bad outcome per se. However, if sites observe that alumni are employed in relatively low-skilled and low-paying occupations despite training for other jobs, site staff may wish to reconsider aspects of the training they offer. In such cases, open-ended questions to alumni about their job experiences or their experiences searching for work may provide helpful context to staff. Finally, sites should collect information on **current or past military experience,** in a manner that distinguishes **active versus reserve component** service. Documenting the **military occupation(s)** and the **amount of military training received** would also be helpful.

Data Pertinent to the Other Core Components of ChalleNGe

We recommend that sites expand the outcomes they measure and collect data on the remaining core components of ChalleNGe. All sites emphasize all eight core components, but the ways in which they emphasize the components and weave them through the curriculum vary across sites. For these reasons, different sites may elect to collect somewhat different information. However, we suggest that the information include **aspects of the eight core components that lie outside of educational attainment and labor force participation.** This information will help program staff to understand more about how alumni interact in their communities and may provide additional information about how sites are meeting their mission. Examples include various **measures of civic and community engagement, physical activity, physical and mental well-being, family formation, and living arrangements**. Specific examples of data to collect could include the extent to which **alumni volunteer or take part in other civic activities** (such as voting), the extent to which the **alumni have been involved with the legal system**, measures of **physical fitness or physical activity**, other measures of **general health**, and even simple measures of **alumni-stated contentment or happiness**. There are many existing survey questions that cover these topics and would allow a comparison between ChalleNGe alumni and other groups.

In Appendix C, we offer some examples of existing scales that focus on citizenship, leadership/followership, and service to community. We note that WYA found in its survey that it could easily collect rich information about alumni reflections on their time at ChalleNGe and their overall support for the program simply by including a couple of queries accompanied by open text boxes in its survey.

Time Frame for Measurement of Outcomes

Sites already maintain contact with recent graduates, although mentors often serve as the conduits for information in the year after graduation. The RCT on ChalleNGe collected information for a total of three years after young people were admitted to ChalleNGe (concluding approximately 2.5 years after ChalleNGe graduation and 1.5 years after the mentoring relationship would likely end). This period proved sufficient to see many graduates of ChalleNGe complete their high school education, obtain postsecondary education or formal training, and enter the labor force (although a number of graduates were still pursuing postsecondary education at the time of the final survey).

We recommend a slightly longer period—three years after graduation. We recommend this period to allow sufficient time for successful outcomes to be reported by program graduates or reflected in existing data systems. Programs are awarding high school credits much more frequently today (i.e., the focus on returning to high school is more prevalent), and today's cadets are somewhat younger than those enrolled during the RCT of the mid-2000s, suggesting that it may take longer than in years past for successful outcomes to be reported by program graduates or reflected in existing data systems. All else being equal, tracking graduates for a longer time will yield more information—but, given the substantial costs and uncertain value associated with collecting additional information, we recommend a 36-month follow-up period at this point. Some sites are experimenting with longer tracking periods. Their findings may eventually suggest that a longer tracking period is appropriate, but, at this point, the information available suggests that three years is an appropriate window.

The Workforce and Innovation Opportunity Act (WIOA) umbrella funds several relatively large programs with a focus on workforce development; most WIOA programs collect very similar outcome measures.[7] The measures are focused mostly on skill gain, credential attainment, education and employment rates, and median earnings. The education, employment, and earnings measures are collected several times over the first year after program completion.

Job Corps is also funded by WIOA, but, as a separate program with a large footprint that also focuses on workforce development, Job Corps is arguably the most similar to ChalleNGe. Like ChalleNGe, Job Corps is a multisite residential program with wraparound services; Job Corps serves a broader age range than ChalleNGe, and the program is means-tested, admitting only those whose household incomes fall below a threshold. Job Corps collects somewhat different information than other WIOA programs, measuring the effectiveness of recruiting and retention efforts, achievement of qualifications and credentials, success of workforce transition, and the extent to which each site is meeting its goals. Job Corps measures change periodically, and, as in other WIOA programs, the Job Corps measures are combined into a single, site-specific measure.

While these other large youth programs provide some lessons for ChalleNGe, their approach also offers some cautions. WIOA programs' measures focus almost exclusively on work and career readiness, including specific measures of credentials and education obtained after leaving the WIOA program, as well as data on earnings. Similar measures would be helpful for the ChalleNGe program, but, given ChalleNGe's broader focus on the eight core components, collecting only workforce and education data would not allow ChalleNGe to measure effectiveness at meeting the program's overall mission. Also, while the WIOA site-level measures offer advantages to those who oversee multiple sites, a head-to-head comparison that does not take into account the many contextual factors discussed in Appendix A could produce misleading results.

Interpreting Results in Measuring Long-Term Outcomes

The goal in measuring long-term outcomes is to determine whether the ChalleNGe program is meeting its mission. But how do we know when those who have completed ChalleNGe have the values, skills, education, and discipline necessary for success?

Measuring educational attainment provides a straightforward answer to one aspect of this question. Given the program's target population, almost all cadets are not on track to complete high school prior to entering ChalleNGe. While some cadets probably would have completed high school without ChalleNGe, a substantial fraction of young people do not graduate from high school, and all available evidence suggests that cadets are drawn from this group (examples of this evidence include admission requirements and qualitative information collected on site visits). Thus, evidence that many or most alumni graduate from high school, and that some or many attend postsecondary school, should be considered central to demon-

[7] See Appendix B for a more detailed discussion and descriptions of specific WIOA measures.

strating that the program is meeting at least a portion of its mission.[8] Tracking employment and earnings will be key to determining the overall economic wellbeing of alumni and to demonstrating whether the program is meeting another portion of its mission.

The central principle behind our guidance on measuring long-term outcomes is that the program should be able to *roughly* replicate some of the findings from the earlier ChalleNGe experiment (the RCT; Bloom, Gardenhire-Crooks, and Mandsager, 2009). An RCT offers the "gold standard" of program evidence—but RCTs are very expensive to run and produce results only after a long analytic period, when one considers the time required to plan an RCT, recruit sites to take part, and recruit both participants and members of the control group. Also, running an RCT requires excluding some young people from the program (they form the control group).[9] For these reasons, we do *not* recommend repeating the previous ChalleNGe RCT.

However, it would be very helpful to have a control group of sorts to help determine program effectiveness. To this end, RAND researchers have developed a series of benchmark measures based on publicly available data (Edwards, 2020). These measures use multiple nationally representative databases to provide information about the outcomes we might expect among young people. Comparing outcomes from these databases with the outcomes observed among ChalleNGe participants can provide information about program effectiveness.[10] The benchmarks will also be helpful to program staff as they form their expectations for graduates' performance. To offer some specific examples, benchmarks on compa-

[8] The results of the ChalleNGe RCT indicated that about one-third of cadets completed high school, and nearly half completed a GED (Bloom, Gardenhire-Crooks, and Mandsager, 2009). Those who attended ChalleNGe were substantially more likely to be employed, but they earned only about 15 percent more per week. These differences were sufficient, when combined, to produce a positive return on investment (ROI) (see Millenky et al., 2011, especially page ES-6, Table ES.1). Note also that the RCT was defined as an *intent to treat* program group—some in this group did not complete the ChalleNGe program. Thus, the measures of educational attainment were likely somewhat higher among ChalleNGe graduates. While the ROI varied somewhat according to assumptions employed (such as future discount rates), the ROI appeared to be higher when wages were estimated using a more recent sample of young workers (see Perez-Arce et al., 2012).

[9] Finally, while RCTs generally are considered superior to other approaches, there is evidence that this may not be the case in every circumstance and that some of the requirements necessary for validity can be problematic in a variety of conditions; see the series of articles presented in Kawachi, Subramanian, and Mowat, 2018.

[10] A slightly different version of an RCT, sometimes called a *low-cost RCT*, depends on using an administrative database to form a control group from otherwise similar people who do not participate. While sample selection is always a worry, this option can provide practical information for some types of programs. However, the United States does not maintain the type of database that would be necessary to form such a control group (specifically, a database of students who are struggling in traditional high school). RAND's benchmark study (Edwards, 2020) provides one option for forming a rough comparison group. Such analysis will not result in a formal ROI calculation, both because there is no formal control group and because there is no consideration of social aspects of costs and benefits, such as tax revenues and associated deadweight losses, social welfare dependency, criminal activity, etc. While there is disagreement surrounding the low-cost RCT language, the term is used among policymakers; see, e.g., Shankar, 2014.

rable populations indicate that average earnings among young people without a high school diploma are quite modest, and arrests are not rare. This type of information can help program staff understand and explain the outcomes of graduates.

For a program to have a positive benefit-cost ratio (in other words, to be *cost-effective*), the program must be *effective* in terms of outcomes (participants must have measurably better outcomes than similar people who did not take part in the program), *and* the program's costs must be less than its benefits. For example, a program could be effective—it could raise participants' earnings by a modest but substantive amount—and yet the program might not be cost-effective if the costs of raising participants' earnings are more than the current and (discounted) future earnings increases. After sites collect long-term outcome information, reestimating the benefit-cost ratio of the ChalleNGe program would be possible, with appropriate caveats depending on how results are benchmarked. In most cases, we recommend that this estimation be carried out at the program level, not the site level. Here, too, collecting information from cadets who did *not* complete ChalleNGe would be valuable.

Path Forward

This chapter lays out a framework for determining how to measure and what to measure regarding the long-term outcomes of young people who complete ChalleNGe. However, sites have considerable freedom in determining a path forward that makes sense for them, as long as they measure outcomes in a defensible manner.

We recommend that each site formulate a plan for measuring outcomes, including details about their overall approach (i.e., keeping in contact with each graduate, following up with past graduates through surveys, etc.). Plans may include multiple approaches as appropriate, but all plans should include a list of specific information to be collected. Sites should plan to collect follow-up information on high school completion for all cadets, including receipt of a regular high school diploma or receipt of a GED. Depending on the site and its relationships within a school district or its state, this collection can be done in a variety of ways. All sites should collect detailed information about labor market experiences. We recommend that sites also collect information about family formation and other aspects of graduates' lives that are especially salient. Information need not be collected each month, and the frequency may depend on the outcome. For example, enrollment queries could occur a few times per year, while employment queries might occur more often.

In general, sites should consider collecting information reasonably frequently to preserve the relationship with the graduate. Spending time and effort socializing cadets and their families to the idea of postgraduation data collection during the program will likely pay large dividends in the postgraduation period. We recommend that sites track graduates for three years. Some sites may wish to track graduates for longer periods or to periodically survey graduates who completed the program more than three years ago. This is likely to yield valuable information.

Finally, determining program success will require comparing graduates' outcomes with those of a control group (an otherwise similar group of young people who did not complete ChalleNGe). We lay out some ideas for this but also note that following up with some of the young people who applied to but did not attend ChalleNGe could yield very valuable information; this effort would require substantial resources and should occur at the program level, not the site level. Sites should use the absolute level of high school completion (if applicable), the absolute level of postsecondary education, measures of income, and comparisons with the benchmark study (Edwards, 2020) to demonstrate effectiveness in meeting the mission and to make adjustments to programs as required.

CHAPTER SIX

Conclusions and Recommendations

In this chapter, we summarize conclusions from our research and analyses on the ChalleNGe program over the past four years. We also lay out a series of recommendations focused on developing measures of longer-term outcomes. The ultimate goal is to provide guidance to the ChalleNGe program as sites seek to measure progress in meeting the program's mission of positively intervening in the lives of young people.

Conclusions

The ChalleNGe program has an ambitious mission. This mission is well-defined, and all the available evidence suggests that the program and the model are well-suited to meeting this mission. Existing evidence also indicates that the program is effective in the sense that participants have quite different outcomes than otherwise similar young people. The program is also cost-effective; participants' eventual earnings are substantially larger than program costs, even given the discounting required to compare current program costs with future earnings.

The existing evidence on ChalleNGe's effectiveness and cost-effectiveness comes from a study that occurred over a decade ago among a subset of program sites, and it is possible that the findings may not hold true today (Bloom, Gardenhire-Crooks, and Mandsager, 2009). On the other hand, changes in the program during the intervening years may have made the program *more* cost-effective than in the past. First, sites have moved increasingly toward a model that includes credit recovery (versus an exclusive focus on preparation for the GED). Those who complete high school earn more than otherwise similar workers who do not, and those who earn a GED often do not complete additional education.[1] Achieving a GED may continue to be a sensible choice for some cadets, but the overall shift toward high school credits is likely to increase the cost-effectiveness of the program. Second, as some ChalleNGe sites have made this shift, the overall high school graduation rate in the United States has increased sharply (Harris et al., 2020). This change has meant a sharp decrease in the number of potential

[1] The essential cite is Cameron and Heckman, 1993, but also see Jepsen, Mueser, and Troske, 2017, on the modest effects of the GED on college attendance and course completion, as well as Millenky et al., 2011, for the educational attainment of ChalleNGe graduates who generally left the program with a GED.

ChalleNGe cadets. To be clear, at any time there are still well over 1 million young people in the United States who are not making progress toward high school completion. But as school districts have focused increasingly on developing alternative programs with the goal of keeping more young people enrolled, the typical ChalleNGe applicant may have more barriers to success than was the case in the past. This observation is consistent with information that we have gathered on our site visits—for example, program staff report that cadets currently are more likely to face mental or behavioral health challenges.[2] This change, too, could mean that the ChalleNGe program, with its whole-person approach, is even better-suited to work with the current population than was the case when the program was developed.

We also note that context matters: ChalleNGe sites exist and operate within vastly different environments. Such factors as local labor markets and cost differences, as well as state and local education policies and other state policies, influence sites in ways that are not always obvious. For these reasons, we recognize that policy recommendations may need to be tailored as appropriate. Below, we lay out a series of flexible policy recommendations with these differences in mind.

Program sites currently collect and report data as required in the cooperative agreement, with a few sites collecting additional information. All sites have reported data to the RAND team on a yearly basis. We recognize that, in some cases, the data reporting required for the past four annual reports has required substantial resources—and the reported data to date have included only elements that the sites are already collecting. In all cases, collecting the information required to measure long-term outcomes will require additional resources. Moreover, sites need support to improve on the current data that they collect on the process portion of the logic model (inputs, activities, outputs). While sites provide useful information on whether inputs are available and activities are taking place, the quality and robustness of the inputs and activities are also important factors to consider, as outlined in the gaps section of Chapter Four. There are many options or models available for these data collection needs, which we outline here. We discuss and contrast these options as part of our recommendations, below.

Recommendations

ChalleNGe sites document a great deal of information about their short-term activities. Traditionally (and appropriately), sites have emphasized a variety of measures, including the number of graduates, the amount of community service performed, scores on standardized tests taken while attending ChalleNGe, and the extent to which graduates are registered to vote. However, measuring the extent to which ChalleNGe is meeting its mission will require collection of additional information—better measures of the quality of the process indica-

[2] For more information on ChalleNGe support for cadets with mental or behavioral health challenges, see Chan and Trail, 2021.

tors, such as measures of contact hours, cadet engagement and learning in the classroom, as well as information documenting graduates' long-term outcomes. In this section, we provide data collection strategies for the program to consider, along with some recommendations on what types of information to collect.

Each Site Should Choose the Data Collection Strategy or Strategies Most Appropriate to the Site Context

As discussed in the previous chapter, there are several major strategies for collecting information on graduates: Collect information from all graduates on an ongoing basis by maintaining contact with them postgraduation; periodically survey graduates; or use existing information in state- or national-level databases to measure outcomes. These choices are not necessarily exclusionary; for example, combining a strategy to maintain contact with and periodically collect data from current graduates with efforts to survey past graduates could make sense for some sites.

In earlier sections of this report, we document some of the differences across sites, in terms of both program focus and external factors. Given the different data collection strategies available and the variation in program focus, resources, and external factors, there is no single data collection strategy that is likely to be the dominant choice for all sites. Instead, *we recommend that each site consider focus, resources, and factors when determining the data collection strategy (or strategies) that are most appropriate within the site's context.*

Regardless of the strategy used to collect information, being able to store and, more importantly, access and analyze the data collected requires a database of some form. We consider a database to be a tool, rather than a data collection strategy. Without consideration of resource requirements, collecting long-term information on all graduates (or perhaps on all participants) and storing the information in a user-friendly database is preferable to other strategies. But this approach may not be practical in all cases.

And even with such a database, surveys offer an option for collecting specific information that is not included in regular data collection efforts. At this point, roughly 10,000 cadets graduate from ChalleNGe each year, and about 184,000 young people have completed the program since the mid-1990s. The contact information for this group is either nonexistent or very out of date. Thus, to the extent that ChalleNGe staff wish to learn about the long-term outcomes of past graduates, they must first expend resources and time to locate those graduates. In such cases, surveying a subsample of graduates provides an opportunity to learn about long-term outcomes.

We note that providing a modest incentive to those who complete the survey may be an effective way to improve the response rate; working with mentors to help encourage graduates to complete surveys could also be effective for surveys that are carried out within one year of graduation. While using information from a survey of a small group of graduates will always require caveats, the information may still provide value to the program. Surveys can

be developed and carried out with relatively little staff effort, but analyzing survey data is complex (especially if weighting is required).

There are also means of organizing ChalleNGe staff during defined periods to focus on data collection. This is an approach that shows early signs of promise. One site hired an employee to take on this primary responsibility. In contrast, purchasing and maintaining a database represents a substantial upfront cost, as well as some ongoing costs and technical expertise, but this option offers the possibility of automatically generated reports rather than requiring substantial resources for analyses. One site contracted for data analytic support during the early stages of launching a new database; this model could allow a site to begin to use and report data while also building the capacity of ChalleNGe staff to take over responsibilities in the long run.

As individual ChalleNGe sites consider their strategies, the existence and accessibility of national- and state-level data sets may influence their decisions. For example, in a state with a robust postsecondary data system, forming a partnership with research staff at a university may be a sensible strategy for measuring postsecondary educational attainment. Of course, such a strategy will require appropriate data use permissions and security.

The optimal strategy may change over time. For example, a site may decide to survey current graduates for immediate information on long-term outcomes but also to put in place a strategy and the resources required to maintain contact with all graduates going forward. In this case, the site may decide to discontinue surveys after demonstrating the capacity to maintain contact with most or all graduates. In some cases, sites may decide to outsource some data collection.

All Sites Should Discuss the Importance of Data Collection with Cadets and Parents

However each site decides to collect information, we recommend that all sites *socialize the data collection with cadets and parents* (as well as continuing to socialize these efforts with mentors). Sites should communicate the importance of data collection efforts and could also consider appropriate incentives to graduates, parents, or mentors who keep in contact. In general, improving mentor engagement will be helpful to these efforts. Our ongoing pilot project may provide additional relevant recommendations in the future.

Site and Program Staff Should Budget for Data Collection Now

Long-term outcome data can be collected in a variety of ways, but all approaches will require resources. While we have no concrete estimate of the amount of time required, one site that has begun to systematically collect information on long-term outcomes from all graduates has indicated that the effort requires less than one full-time-equivalent staff member. *We recommend that site and program staff begin to plan and budget for this effort now, and we expect that in many cases the amount budgeted should be considerably more than the amount required for one staff member.* A first step would be to identify specific long-term outcome measures, identify preferred methods to collect the information, and begin to form an estimate in terms of staff time and other resources required.

All Sites Should Collect Data on Graduates' Educational Attainment, Labor Force Experience, and Progress on Other Core Components

As discussed above, *we recommend collecting specific information on educational attainment* (credential attainment—completion of the GED certificate, completion of a high school diploma, completion of standard industry-recognized certificates or similar credentials, and completion of college courses or programs). In particular, we recommend that sites awarding high school credits as part of a credit recovery program track their graduates' success in receiving high school diplomas; these sites should make efforts to understand and help cadets overcome any barriers that seem to prevent high school completion. *We also recommend collecting specific information on labor force experience*—hours worked, pay, job turnover, existence of benefits, and industry and occupation. Finally, *we recommend collecting additional information to track progress in the other core components.* This could include information on family formation, civic participation, health and well-being, etc.[3]

Sites Should Collect Data for Three Years Postgraduation

Collecting information over a three-year postgraduation period would allow time for many graduates to continue or complete their education and to settle into the job market. The RCT that was used to demonstrate ChalleNGe's effectiveness tracked cadets for this period. Therefore, tracking for a three-year period would also allow sites to form a rough benchmark against the earlier RCT results. However, programs today are more likely than those in the past to offer credit recovery; in these cases, graduates move home and return to their previous high schools. A survey of graduates from WYA demonstrated that many graduates required at least two years to complete high school. If staff find that most graduates have not yet completed their education at the end of the three-year window, then tracking graduates for a longer period of time may be advisable.

The ChalleNGe Program Should Invest in a Single, Consistent Administrative Database

Our final recommendation is that the ChalleNGe program invest in a single, consistent administrative database. Having a single database that all sites accessed would allow consistent data collection, would very likely increase the quality—and thereby usability—of the data, and would free the sites from spending substantial resources collecting required information.

3 Social desirability bias—the habit or tendency of answering questions in a way that emphasizes positive outcomes and behaviors—has the potential to bias survey data. Developing questions that feature neutral, socially acceptable answers can be helpful; see, e.g., Karp and Brockington, 2014.

This issue is discussed in Chapter Four, as lack of systemization and consistency in collecting data can compromise data quality by introducing errors at various stages of the data collection and management process. Instead, required information could be accessed centrally. The Cadet Tracker database, which is used by most programs, may offer a model for this. However, we recommend that program staff gain a good understanding of Cadet Tracker's weaknesses and limitations as well as its strengths, and of the reasons why some sites do not use the system, prior to determining how to standardize data collection. For example, some sites have reported during our visits that entering data into Cadet Tracker can be time-consuming due to issues with the system's speed and capacity. Also, under the current setup, sites cannot easily compare their outcomes with the national average; such comparisons could be very helpful to sites.

Of course, a national database would need strong security features. We recognize that the ChalleNGe program must meet myriad data requirements; some of these requirements are relevant due to DoD oversight, but state requirements differ as well—and, in general, programs that include minor participants face strict data security requirements. An off-the-shelf system could offer some advantages in terms of technical support.

A single administrative database would offer possibilities for increased efficiency in several different ways. First, automating some data collection (such as TABE scores) might be possible. Of course, collecting long-term information on graduates would remain a time-intensive task. However, with a single administrative database, it would be possible to contract with an external organization to collect long-term placement data. Having case managers maintain some oversight during the data collection could be sensible, but contracting out the actual data collection could result in more-thorough data and could reserve site staff for other duties. This could also result in fewer data quality issues (currently, data collection and entry generally are additional tasks assigned to staff—along with many other tasks).

With a single source of data, accessing the required information for annual reports could occur centrally (currently, data calls go out to and must be filled by staff at each site). Additionally, matching data on graduates to extant data systems (such as state or national files tracking postsecondary educational attainment or participation in the unemployment compensation system) could be implemented centrally. Aside from potentially saving staff effort, this system could make it possible to glean information on graduates who have moved across state lines. Finally, a well-populated administrative database would, over time, provide the information needed to select a random subsample of graduates (or participants, or nongraduates) for a focused survey or for a panel of participants who are contacted periodically to learn more about their experiences. As mentioned above, such data collection would require substantial permissions and other security features, but it would be possible, and the information could be quite valuable to ChalleNGe. Indeed, such a database could provide information to help the program better target advertising efforts.

Closing Thoughts

We recognize that developing a single administrative database will require time. In the interim, sites should develop a strategy for data collection that is appropriate based on their resources and other constraints. We have provided several recommendations above for how this data collection might be organized. Comparing outcomes with benchmarks described in Edwards, 2020, may help sites to assess their progress.

The ChalleNGe program serves young people who struggle in traditional high schools. Even given the large increase in high school completion over the past decade, many young people still leave school without a credential. The ChalleNGe program is well-positioned to enact positive changes in the lives of participants, but to this point, the program has not systematically measured these changes. Measuring long-term outcomes will allow the program to document progress in meeting its mission and will provide information for staff to make improvements to the program as necessary.

APPENDIX A

Contextual Factors That Influence ChalleNGe Sites

Although the ChalleNGe program model provides a standard structure of operation and expectation (Department of Defense Instruction 1025.8, 2002, superseded 2020; Chief National Guard, 2015), and the individual program sites have many elements in common, we observed substantive variations in the policies, practices, and contexts that influence how each site operates during our site visits. Some of the variation we identified appears to be linked to the site's locale—for example, each site hires from a local labor market and operates within the context of the state's policies on education—but other sources of variation exist as well. Variation in contextual factors across sites may have an impact on how well each site performs its functions. For example, previous research has found that, even after controlling for basic measures of participants' backgrounds and initial preparation, graduation rates significantly differ across sites (Wenger et al., 2008). In this chapter, we discuss several key sources or drivers of variation: geographic proximity and local resources, job market forces and staff compensation and hiring, and state education policy and practice. These factors are recognized by program staff; they were among the most common topics raised by staff during our site visits. These factors have implications for the services and resources that a site can offer to cadets; they also affect the ease or challenge with which supports, staff, and resources can be located. Relevant to this report, these contextual factors will likely explain some of the differences in long-term outcomes across program sites or over time; discounting these factors may limit ChalleNGe's ability to improve program effectiveness and the efficient allocation of program resources in the future. We discuss key contextual factors below and use examples from ChalleNGe sites to illustrate the variation across programs.[1]

Geographic Proximity and Local Resources

The opportunities that ChalleNGe programs are able to offer cadets are influenced by what resources lie within a site's local community or can be accessed with relative ease (e.g., within a

[1] All the data for this chapter were collected by RAND staff during annual site visits from 2016 through 2019. It is possible that some of the program components discussed in what follows have evolved or changed since a site visit was conducted, especially in any cases where policy has required program sites to adapt past practices.

short drive). These opportunities vary substantively by site as program locations, both within and across states, differ. Each ChalleNGe program location falls along a continuum between being in a well-resourced community to being in a community with minimal resources. And, in some cases, what is a geographic benefit for one aspect of the site's operations may be a challenge to other operational aspects. For example, a site that is located near a large city may be able to provide enrichment through field trips but may also be forced to hire from a highly competitive labor market. The geographic factors that we explore in this section include the proximity of a site to external education and training resources; the location of a program relative to major participant recruitment and, subsequently, post-residential placement areas; and the location's desirability and cost for hiring and retaining staff.

External Education and Training Resources

External education and training resources are influenced by the number and type of educational institutions nearby, as well as access to historical sites and other areas that could provide enriching educational experiences. For example, California's Grizzly Youth Academy is in San Luis Obispo, an urban community accessible by two major freeways and home to historic sites and at least one major university. The ChalleNGe program is situated on a military installation, down the street from Cuesta Community College. The staff at Grizzly established a partnership with the community college to enable cadets who are pursuing a GED to concurrently enroll in classes (e.g., goal setting, career planning, and individual advisement). Some students can enroll in CTE programs at Cuesta Community College in the areas of auto mechanics, web design, and broadcasting. Most cadets from this program graduate from ChalleNGe with four college credits. In addition to academic program access, Grizzly's urban location enables the program to offer regular enrichment opportunities, including trips to Hearst Castle, art museums, or local theaters.

A contrast to the abundant education and training resources found near San Luis Obispo is Eagle Lake, Texas. The Texas ChalleNGe Academy is located approximately 50 miles from the outskirts of a major metropolitan area in the state. The Texas program, not for lack of interest, is not able to offer cadets opportunities to enroll in college courses during the residential portion of the program. The program's leadership has looked into establishing a partnership with Texas State Technical College; however, that institution is more than 35 miles away from the site. Even when such a relationship can be developed, it is likely that the partnership will be used to support cadets in identifying opportunities for and successfully transitioning to post-residential life rather than as a partnership that serves cadets during the residential phase. ChalleNGe sites are located in many different types of areas; thus, education and training resources vary substantially between sites. But such resources likely have an impact on cadets' educational experiences and eventual outcomes.

Recruitment and Placement Proximity

The amount of physical territory a program covers to recruit cadets and support graduates influences the way programs operate for both the pre- and post-residential phases. RAND's site visits frequently included conversations regarding the division of labor between the site's recruiters and how program sites maximized recruiting potential. These conversations also focused on the way sites leverage networks within the state for post-residential placement and mentoring.

Programs located in small states or in states with multiple ChalleNGe sites may approach recruitment with different tactics. For example, for Classes 50 and 51, in 2018, New Jersey had three recruiters to cover 8,729 square miles. By contrast, Texas had four recruiters to cover 268,597 square miles. Each Texas recruiter has substantially more territory to cover than a New Jersey recruiter, which can influence the approach to recruitment and the amount of personal interaction between the recruiter and potential applicants and their families. Therefore, Texas recruiters have home bases throughout the state to increase the amount of territory they can cover. The program also uses a pre-admission interview process, which is referred to as a *roadshow*. Teams of staff, including admissions specialists, cadre members, and case managers, travel to conduct screenings and interviews in Dallas–Fort Worth, Houston, San Antonio, Austin, and 700 miles away in El Paso. For potential recruits and families interested in seeing the program site prior to enrolling, Texas hosts a three-week period for families to visit the site if personal time and resources permit.

In Virginia, the Commonwealth ChalleNGe program is located on the southeastern border of the state. The Virginia program leverages relationships and partnerships to ensure that it can reach potential recruits from across the state. The program sets up a booth at the Virginia School Counselor Association annual conference that is held a short distance away. Officials use this conference to inform all school counselors in the state about the program and the types of students the program serves. Virginia's staff have also tapped into the state's 211 system, which is a free service for anyone in Virginia to find local resources. This network gives Commonwealth ChalleNGe connections to the state's Department of Education and Department of Justice that allow ChalleNGe staff to inform staff in those departments about the types of young people Commonwealth ChalleNGe is seeking and how the program serves cadets. Thus, rather than rely solely on three recruiters to connect with each community in the state, this program has built partnerships and relationships that maximize the reach of recruitment within a limited budget.[2]

In the same way that recruitment is influenced by the sheer physical size of a state, so is the work that a program's staff must do to develop relationships and connections to enhance post-residential placement of cadets. For cadets not returning to a hometown high school or other education settings, placement coordinators must be knowledgeable and connected to employment opportunities throughout the entire state. This is particularly challenging in vast states. In some states with multiple sites (such as California), each individual program in a state focuses on a specific portion of the state; this means that program staff have a more manageable task in maintaining connections for placements. However, even in states with less territory, there are cases in which the site is far from many of the population centers;

---

2 The program reported three recruiters in 2017, 2018, and 2019.

this presents challenges in terms of placement. Idaho is an example of such a site; staff indicated that they have put substantial effort into developing and maintaining relationships with employers and community leaders whose communities are a long distance from the site.

Job Market Forces and State Policies for Staff Hiring and Compensation

In the 2019 ChalleNGe report (Constant et al., 2019) and in previous reports, staff turnover has been a point of discussion. In other educational settings, staff retention is linked closely to student learning and overall school performance (Ronfeldt, Loeb, and Wyckoff, 2013). In the 2019 report, staff compensation was offered as a potential explanation for turnover among ChalleNGe staff (Constant et al., 2019). Compensation is not the sole factor driving staff turnover; leadership changes, state regulations regarding position rank or experience, and the natural progression of an individual's career are likely contributors. However, during site visits, the conversation often turns to compensation and competing with the surrounding or statewide labor markets for hiring.

At one of the sites we visited,[3] staff reported that ChalleNGe academic instructors historically were paid a salary commensurate with a public-school teacher who had six or seven years of experience. In recent years, public school teachers statewide received a salary increase. The ChalleNGe instructor salary is now commensurate with a brand-new public-school teacher or approximately 90 percent of the salary of a public-school teacher who has six or seven years of experience. This is true for ChalleNGe academic instructors at this site even when they have 15 or more years of teaching experience. The academic instructors at ChalleNGe sites have an immediate job alternative in the public school system if they hold a state certification. Consequently, ChalleNGe sites have to compete with the external, public labor market to hire and retain instructors, which is more difficult to do when the ChalleNGe compensation package does not equally recognize and reward professional experience.

Issues of competitive compensation for cadre follow a similar theme. At multiple sites, staff reported that the cadre are paid hourly, and the pay rate is low relative to the local community and low given the demands of the position. The current position funding level means that the site is attracting young individuals (e.g., 24 or 25 years old) fresh out of the military, with limited or no experience working with at-risk youth. To further complicate matters, it is not unusual for a program site to have cadre openings or staff who are pulled away for their required Reserve or National Guard training or deployments. The remaining cadre must pick up additional shifts and responsibilities to ensure that the site has sufficient adults per youth at all times. Program staff across several sites reported that this combination of pay that is not on par with the local community and additional shift requirements can lead to staff burnout, which may further increase staff turnover. During one site visit, a group of cadre reported

[3] Due to the sensitive nature of salary information, both the program site and the dollar amount of salaries are masked.

that they had worked 14 days straight without a day off to cover a combination of open staff positions and current staff away for training.

Even in communities where staff compensation is commensurate with the local community's salaries and cost of living, there are other conditions that affect staff hiring and retention. Some program sites are in communities that have limited housing and resources (e.g., public schools, community resources) available for staff. This means that staff have extended commutes to their jobsite. In other cases, where the site location is desirable to staff and local resources are abundant, staff report that the Basic Allowance for Housing often does not adequately cover rent. These living conditions factor into staff hiring and staff retention.

The final staff contextual factor that we highlight is the hiring process itself. Each state, and therefore almost every program site, has a different set of regulations and processes for hiring staff. Some sites can manage most of the hiring process in house. This means that they post the job opening, screen and interview applicants, and can hire someone to fill the position in relatively short order. At other sites, leadership does not have direct oversight of the hiring process. For example, at the Indiana Hoosier Youth ChalleNGe Academy (HYCA), all staff are state employees, so the state oversees advertising, review of the candidate pool, establishment of pay scales, etc. Each ChalleNGe job posting must comply with the state regulations, meaning that the posting must be available for a set length of time before candidates can be screened, interviewed, or hired. In some cases, this means that viable and desirable job candidates are identified early in the hiring process but that an offer cannot be made until weeks later. The hiring delays can create situations in which the best candidates are no longer available when hiring is allowed. This means not only that the site is not getting its top-choice candidate but also that the hiring process extends beyond the initially planned time frame because a new search needs to be opened and the hiring clock resets. Other sites described very similar hiring processes.

State Education Policy and Practice

There are nearly as many approaches to academic instruction across ChalleNGe as there are ChalleNGe program sites. This is due, in part, to state policy contexts, as well as the ways in which programs have elected to approach the academic core component. Providing a complete review of the differences in academic instruction across sites is beyond the scope of this research. Instead, we provide an overview of some of the ways in which state policy and practice intersect with standardized testing and with sites' academic instruction. We begin by discussing some of the differences across standardized tests; we then describe briefly the various academic foci at programs, with an emphasis on how state policies influence these differences.

High School Equivalency Exams and Diplomas

Each site makes use of at least one standardized assessment. These assessments differ in various ways.[4] The GED was the only high school equivalency assessment option for ChalleNGe when the program began (Zinth, 2015). In 2014, the High School Equivalency Test (HiSET) and the Test Assessing Secondary Completion (TASC) assessments were introduced as alternatives (ETS HiSET, 2020; McGraw-Hill Communications Team, 2014). Each of these assessments is a valid assessment for students to secure their *recognized equivalent* of a high school diploma, though which assessment is recognized varies by state.

Most ChalleNGe sites offer high school equivalency exams as part of their program and track the number of cadets who successfully meet all exam requirements during the residential phase. As part of this process, each site uses one of the assessments approved within its state. For example, the California sites can choose any of the three exams (i.e., GED, HiSET, TASC) for their cadets, while Montana administers only the HiSET, and West Virginia administers only the TASC. These examinations do not cover identical material, and each is aligned to a somewhat different standard; therefore, a cadet who passes one of the examinations may not pass one of the others.[5] Additionally, each state sets its own threshold for passing.[6] Finally, each state has different regulations regarding eligibility criteria to sit for the exam.[7] In some cases, the differences in eligibility criteria are linked to the state's compulsory schooling requirements; many states require students to attend school until the age of 18, while others allow students to leave school under various circumstances.[8] To summarize, having passed a given exam guarantees slightly different minimum levels of academic achievement, depending on the state.

---

[4] All sites use the TABE as a means of measuring or tracking progress. For more information on the TABE, see Wenger et al., 2017, or TABE Test, undated.

[5] The GED and HiSET are aligned to the National College and Career Readiness Standards for Adult Education ("High School Equivalency Assessments Comparison of Tests," undated; ETS HiSET, 2020). The TASC is aligned to these same standards, as well as to the Next Generation Science Standards and the Social Studies National Framework.

[6] California's passing score on the GED is a 145, whereas New Jersey requires a score of 150. These states, respectively, require an 8 and a 9 on the HiSET exams to pass (New Jersey Department of Education, 2019).

[7] California places restrictions on who is eligible to test for a GED, with most individuals needing to be 18 years old or within 60 days of their 18th birthday. Even when a California resident successfully passes all components of the exam, the equivalency certificate is withheld until the individual reaches his or her 18th birthday (GED Testing Service, undated-a). Michigan, by contrast, has written into its policy an exemption for graduates of the Michigan National Guard Youth ChalleNGe Academy; any program graduate who is at least 16 years of age and no longer enrolled in high school is eligible to test (GED Testing Service, undated-b).

[8] Compulsory schooling laws can have substantial effects, even across generations (Oreopoulos, Page, and Stevens, 2006).

Status of Instructional Program

We found that most program sites' academic components can be classified into four approaches, with some programs offering more than one approach: (1) Operate or partner with a fully accredited high school, (2) operate an accredited education program, (3) provide students with options for credit recovery and/or credit accumulation (i.e., courses they can transfer to their local high school after graduating from ChalleNGe), and (4) deliver instruction in preparation for a high school equivalency credential such as the GED, HiSET, or TASC. In each case, the state's specific policies are a key factor as the site determines which pathways to offer. Below, we discuss several examples of how sites offer various academic components within state contexts.

One example of a partnership with a fully accredited high school is Oklahoma's Thunderbird Academy. In 2015, Thunderbird Academy began a partnership with EPIC charter schools, a state-funded, virtual, accredited charter school. Each cadet can choose a personalized pathway through the EPIC program: credit recovery, completion of a high school diploma, or instruction in preparation for the GED. Students who do not complete a credential (high school diploma or GED) while at Thunderbird Academy can either remain enrolled in the EPIC program after their time at ChalleNGe or transfer the completed credits back to their local high school.

The EPIC charter school program comes with benefits for Thunderbird Academy, including Chromebooks for every student and a Learning Fund of at least $800 per cadet, which can be spent on enrichment activities (e.g., field trips) or curriculum and academic-related materials (e.g., novels required for coursework). EPIC also sends state-certified teachers to the program site twice or more each week to support cadets, at no cost to ChalleNGe. Thunderbird Academy also employs five academic instructors, in addition to any EPIC-provided teachers, to oversee the academic portion of the day and assist students in their learning. While this setup has many advantages for Thunderbird staff and cadets, the local schools in Oklahoma lose the student enrollment when a cadet enrolls at Thunderbird. This includes the school losing any associated per-student funding; staff reported that this may create some reluctance by those public schools to suggest or support Thunderbird Academy for struggling students.

The loss of per-student funding is common across programs and does not depend on the program partnering with an accredited high school, but it does not happen in all cases. For example, cadets who participate in any of Louisiana's three program sites remain enrolled in their parish (i.e., local) high school while enrolled at ChalleNGe. When a cadet attends a Louisiana ChalleNGe program, their parish school does not lose any per-student expenditures associated with that student. Rather, the local school maintains the student enrollment and the associated funding, the cadet goes to ChalleNGe to receive additional support and instruction, and, ideally, the student returns to the home institution better prepared for coursework and/or on track for high school graduation. Thus, Louisiana programs are able to partner and support local schools, rather than competing for students, which may ease recruitment challenges and increase the likelihood of schools supporting student enrollment in ChalleNGe.

Additionally, Louisiana's programs have recently started a new pathway within their academic component. Historically, all cadets were provided instruction in preparation for the HiSET (and prior to the emergence of the HiSET, cadets prepared for the GED). While HiSET preparation remains the most common instructional program offered by ChalleNGe sites in the state, each of the state's three sites has undertaken credit recovery and course choice (CR/CC) options for cadets. *Credit recovery* allows cadets to repeat courses that they previously did not complete successfully at their local school, and *course choice* allows students to take new courses that are required for high school graduation; each type of course credit can be taken back to the cadet's parish high school. Thus, when all course requirements have been completed, the cadet receives a high school diploma.

Notably, these new educational options are resource intensive. Prior to a cadet starting the CR/CC pathway, there must be an established agreement from the student's parish high school, the cadet's parent or guardian, and the ChalleNGe site. Louisiana's education coordinator works with all interested cadets and families prior to the first day of ChalleNGe to ensure that all the necessary documentation is processed. Furthermore, cadets in this pathway require more academic time than the HiSET-focused instruction, and the program is offered using internet-based software, so programs must procure sufficient technology to support the CR/CC pathway.

Indiana, like many other states, has seen a proliferation of charter schools and other alternative educational programs that provide additional options for the ChalleNGe target population. The leadership at the HYCA reported that they inquired about establishing a charter school because program leadership had seen, in their community, a stigma related to having a GED as compared with the traditional high school diploma. Unfortunately, HYCA was told that it does not meet the charter requirements in Indiana, because cadets would require substantially more instructional time than is currently structured into the program, and the site does not administer mandated state-standardized testing. The HYCA thus offers academic instruction that supports preparation for the TASC. Moreover, all students at HYCA will take the TASC—which is unique to Indiana; many other program sites will allow cadets to take the GED/HiSET/TASC only when they demonstrate likelihood of passing, based on TABE or GED practice test scores. Another unique feature of Indiana's program is that any cadets who participate in HYCA are required, by the state's education department, to change their local school enrollment status to *homeschool*. These cadets are no longer enrolled in the public school system, and they are not enrolled in a program that offers credits that transfer back to their local high school. Therefore, these cadets lack a clear path to obtaining a high school diploma. This policy also likely disadvantages cadets in terms of eventual military enlistment, as enrollment of homeschool graduates is somewhat more restricted than that of traditional high school graduates.

APPENDIX B

How Similar Youth Programs Approach Data Collection and Outcomes Measurement

ChalleNGe is one in an array of programs targeted toward youth who fall under the broad umbrella of *at-risk*. Some of these programs work with youth before they leave school, encouraging regular high school completion; others work with students who have dropped out, hoping to increase attainment of or reenrollment in school for a high school diploma; and others work with individuals who have dropped out of high school and graduates who are looking to obtain needed job skills. These programs vary on myriad dimensions, from setting (e.g., residential or nonresidential) to financing (i.e., where funding comes from). Regardless of these differences, programs geared toward populations like ChalleNGe cadets collect program and outcome data on their participants. In this section, we discuss the measures collected by a set of these programs. This information provides ChalleNGe an opportunity to understand where its own data practices align and explore alternative or additional types of measures that could help shape ChalleNGe data collection for the future.

Youth Programs Under WIOA

WIOA (Pub. L. 113-128, 2014) was enacted in July 2014 and succeeded the Workforce Investment Act of 1998 (Pub. L. 105-220, 1998) as the primary federal workforce development legislation and largest source of training funds. Of the many new or changed aspects of WIOA relevant to this discussion, WIOA mandates that the programs within the WIOA umbrella of funding—Adult, Dislocated Worker, Youth, Adult Education and Family Literacy Act, Employment Services, and Vocational Rehabilitation programs—collect *Primary Indicators of Performance* (U.S. Department of Labor, Employment and Training Administration Advisory System, 2017). The WIOA youth programs include YouthBuild, Reentry Employment Opportunities, and Youth Program.

The same six measures, collected from the same or similar data, are used to gauge success across the portfolio of WIOA-funded programs. For this reason, these measures are referred to as the WIOA common measures. These measures include measurable skill gains; credential attainment; employment and education rate, second quarter after exit; median earnings, second quarter after exit; employment and education rate, fourth quarter after exit; and effectiveness in serving employers. The last of these measures is a new indicator, currently

being piloted to identify the best measurement approach, to assess the goal of having workforce programs serve the needs of the business community. Notably, the definitions of the six common measures are modified to account for the population served by WIOA's youth programs. We summarize the common measures as they are measured for youth programs in Table B.1.

In many ways, ChalleNGe sites collect similar data elements to those needed to construct WIOA common measures, but ChalleNGe data are not currently aggregated to assess performance in parallel ways to WIOA programs. For example, ChalleNGe sites keep track of an individual cadet's academic progress through the residential phase, including whether the cadet is in a pathway toward credit recovery, GED attainment, or a high school diploma (where applicable). In addition, sites also monitor nonacademic progress, such as occupational skill classes, driver's license exams, or successful completion of life skills curricula (e.g., a financial education module). These types of progress are similar to the aim of the WIOA's measurable skill gains measure.

Given that ChalleNGe encompasses myriad education offerings (both within and across sites), it is difficult to imagine that a single measure of academic or skills progress would be appropriate. Moreover, a single measure would likely create "cream-skimming" incentive

TABLE B.1
Summary of WIOA Measures of Primary Indicators of Performance

Measure	Time When Measured	Description
Measurable skill gains	During the program	The share of participants who are in an education or training program that leads to a credential, or who are achieving measurable skills gains—documented academic, technical, or occupational progress
Credential attainment	During the program and up to 1 year after program participation ends	The share of participants enrolled in education or training programs who attain a high school diploma (or equivalent) or a postsecondary credential
Employment and education rate, 2nd quarter after exit	4–6 months after program participation ends	The share of participants who are in unsubsidized employment, education, or training
Median earnings, 2nd quarter after exit	4–6 months after program participation ends	The median earnings of participants who are in unsubsidized employment
Employment and education rate, 4th quarter after exit	10–12 months after program participation ends	The share of participants who are in unsubsidized employment, education, or training
Effectiveness in serving employers	No set time period	• The share of participants in unsubsidized employment in quarters 2 and 4 who are with the same employer • The number or share of employers who employ more than one program participant (at any time or over time) • The share of all employers in the state who employ program participants

SOURCE: U.S. Department of Labor, Employment and Training Administration Advisory System, 2017.

effects—to try to recruit only individuals who are likely to succeed or to offer only programs that are less challenging and easier to pass. However, an array of measures that span all academic tracks can be extremely useful. A site could keep track of, for example, (a) average number of GED subject tests passed by GED-prep students, (b) average number of credits recovered by credit-recovery students, and (c) share of students in an occupation or skills module who complete the module.

The WIOA programs have a considerable advantage when producing summary measures that ChalleNGe sites do not. WIOA programs collect and verify wage and employer information primarily using administrative wage records from a state's unemployment insurance system, which can retrieve information about a worker's quarterly earnings and employer identification number with the use of a Social Security number.

Finally, WIOA requires programs to report on how well they are serving their states through the measure Effectiveness in Serving Employers. This indicator is likely not well suited to the ChalleNGe context. WIOA programs are often much larger than ChalleNGe (in number of individuals served) and have a broader mission, so the ways of measuring employer effectiveness (e.g., the share of employers in a state that are served) are not all appropriate or feasible for a program like ChalleNGe. But the other two means of measuring employer effectiveness could be produced by ChalleNGe sites: the share of employed cadets who have the same employer for the year after the program and the number of employers who employ more than one cadet. The latter, in particular, can also help with direct post-residential placement aid for sites.

Job Corps

Of all existing programs geared toward young individuals, the natural comparable program with ChalleNGe is Job Corps, a federally funded, multisite residential education and training program run through the Department of Labor for low-income youth aged 16–24. Job Corps was established by the 1964 Economic Opportunity Act and eventually brought under the umbrella of training programs included in WIOA.[1] Much like ChalleNGe, Job Corps participants live on site and participate in education and training programs, though the age group is much wider (16–24 versus 16–18 years old), participants must meet low-income requirements for eligibility to participate, and the length of residential stay is not uniform. Job Corps is also a much larger program, operating in more states than ChalleNGe, with more sites per state, and larger numbers of participants each year (U.S. Department of Labor, Employment and Training Administration Advisory System, 2014).

Although part of WIOA, Job Corps has a much more comprehensive and dynamic performance measurement system than that mandated by the WIOA common measures (U.S. Department of Labor, Office of Job Corps, 2021); Job Corps centers meet multiple report-

---

[1] Governance of Job Corps and all existing federal job training programs was consolidated into a unified structure by Pub. L. 93-203, 1973, and subsequently directed by Pub. L. 97-300, 1982,, Pub. L. 105-220, 1998, and Pub. L. 113-128, 2014, (WIOA).

ing requirements that span various, overlapping time periods. The basic structure of performance system is that each Job Corps site produces four report cards each program year as well as in rolling 12-month windows. In 2018, the Job Corps performance management system underwent a major redesign. It is instructive for ChalleNGe that Job Corps' performance metrics are designed to answer enumerated program questions:

1. Are Job Corps students effectively recruited and retained?
2. While enrolled in Job Corps, do students achieve fundamental qualifications and credentials that could lead to either a career path with opportunity for advancement and economic stability or higher education?
3. Are Job Corps students successfully transitioning into the workforce, enrolling in additional education or training, or entering the military after they leave the program?
4. How is each Job Corps contractor (Center, Outreach and Admissions [OA], and Career Transition Services [CTS]) performing compared with the established annual performance goals and other contractors (U.S. Department of Labor, Office of Job Corps, 2021)?

Combined, the four report cards that Job Corps sites produce provide comprehensive answers to these questions. Notably, Job Corps reviews and revises performance measures and how the measures are weighted in the overall report cards every year. Table B.2 summarizes the four report cards according to program year 2019 guidance.

Although measuring different aspects of the program, each report card has the same basic structure. First, there are a series of performance measures that are expressed as a metric—for example, the share of participants enrolled in career training. Next, for each measure, there is a stated, site-specific goal that is updated annually, such as the site's target share of participants in career training. Then, all the performance measures are weighted. These weights are percentages that reflect that metric's importance—across all metrics in a report card, the weights sum to 100 percent. Afterward, each measure is rated for performance and then combined with other measures in a weighted sum to express a single, overall rating. Hence, Job Corps' performance system incorporates, in a flexible way, site-specific goals as well as program-wide priorities.

Job Corps' report cards cover each program year, as well as rolling 12-month windows, and each report card is available publicly, in a commitment to transparency and accountability.

Other Youth Programs

WIOA and Job Corps are the large, federal training programs whose performance measures are most applicable to ChalleNGe. However, there are a few other programs whose evaluation methods we reviewed. The first is the *Marion Barry Youth Summer Employment Program* (MBYSEP) in Washington, D.C. MBYSEP is a city-funded program that provides D.C. youth ages 14–24 with subsidized summer jobs with private, public, and nonprofit employers. MBYSEP serves mainly low-income youth, many of whom are homeless. Like ChalleNGe,

TABLE B.2
Summary of Job Corps Report Cards

Report Card	Time When Measured	Description
Center report card	During the program and up to 1 year after program participation ends	The Center report card evaluates overall performance of a site and includes all six WIOA common measures, as well as an additional postprogram wage measure and a measure of postprogram placement quality, such as whether the placement was in the field of skills training of the participant and whether the placement was a full-time position.
Outreach and admissions (OA) report card	During the program	The OA report card evaluates recruiting and retention over a program year or 12-month period. Performance measures include the number of new participants, overall and female, compared with the contracted quota; the number of participants who had to be removed from the program for behavior violations; the number of participants who stayed at least 90 days, and the number of participants who graduated.
CTS report card	Up to 1 year after program participation ends	The CTS report card evaluates postprogram outcomes, including the placement rate, placement quality (measured by whether the placement was either full time or aligned with occupation training received in Job Corps), and 1-year placement outcomes; it is redundant with part of the Center report card.
Career Technical Training (CTT) report card	During the program and up to 1 year after participation ends.	The CTT report card evaluates the technical training offered by the Job Corps program. Performance measures span enrollment and completion in industry-certified training courses and the placement of training completers.

SOURCE: U.S. Department of Labor, Office of Job Corps, 2021.

the program is intended to intervene in the lives of at-risk youth with positive, structured programs, although MBYSEP youth do not receive housing. MBYSEP is annually evaluated by an independent firm (Coles Group, 2019). Much of the program's evaluation is based on a survey administered to youth participants and employers toward the end of each summer. The participant survey asks about overall program satisfaction, alternatives should they not have participated in MBSYEP, satisfaction with the job placement, and their assessment of the skills learned and the benefits of the program.

Check and Connect is a school-based high school dropout prevention program. Students at risk of dropping out are closely monitored in their class performance and assigned an in-person monitor who is part caseworker, reviewing all reports on student performance, and part mentor, providing feedback, coordinating services, and advocating on behalf of the student. The student is systematically monitored for school performance (i.e., *check*) and then works with the monitor to come up with individualized interventions (i.e., *connect*). Monitors are expected to be trained or in training for human services and social work, such as graduate students. Although it is not strictly regarded as a performance measure, Check and Connect has a monthly monitoring form that documents, daily, how the student is doing academically (e.g., number of missing assignments, grades on quizzes or tests) and behaviorally (e.g., tardy, skipped a class, detention) and notes all contact that the monitor has with the student. As part of the form, the contact with students is catalogued by what was discussed among nearly two dozen topics, including behavior, graduation, tutoring, school activities, study skills, and problem solving. Critically, the student discussion with the monitor is not solely the result of a negative student action—that is, conversations with monitors are regular and irrespective of good or bad behavior. Based on the daily performance of the student, the monitor helps develop a plan or response to continually support that student on the path to high school graduation. Evaluations of Check and Connect have found that the combination of detailed, though not necessarily in-depth, student performance measures with frequent, individualized check-ins was the source of the success of the intervention (Sinclair et al., 1998).

Conclusion

The array of youth programs reviewed in this appendix provides insight into the varied approaches to measuring progress and performance in ways that are suited to the context and goals of each of the programs. ChalleNGe, with any new data collection, must consider what data are most critical to best promote understanding of areas of strength, areas for improvement, and the extent to which desired outcomes are being produced for its participants and graduates. While adopting all the measures or data collection approaches in this appendix is not feasible, given program resources, nor is that our intention in providing this information, these data and measure procedures can help ChalleNGe leaders think critically about practices to better inform data collection efforts in the future.

APPENDIX C

Potential Measures of Citizenship, Leadership/Followership, and Service to Community

Here, we provide an overview of potential measures of citizenship, leadership/followership, and service to community. We offer specific information on a few measures and reference other measures that may be relevant to measuring how cadets interact with their communities after completing ChalleNGe. The measures that we include have been used either to evaluate programs similar to ChalleNGe or to examine one of ChalleNGe's core components in an empirical study. All the scales presented are designed to be used in a survey format.

Citizenship

Traditional political activities, such as voting, joining a political party, and working for or donating to a political campaign, are examples of the wide range of citizenship activities engaged in by youth. There are several established measures of citizenship; below, we share a few.

The International Association for the Evaluation of Educational Achievement developed a measure focusing on *conventional citizenship* (Schulz and Sibberns, 2004). The two scales most relevant to ChalleNGe measure citizenship and political action and are presented in Tables C.1 and C.2. The citizenship scale asks respondents to identify the importance of civic behaviors, from not important (1) to very important (4). The political action scale asks respondents to report what actions they will or will not take as an adult. The language in these scales may require updating to better express current notions of citizenship and political participation, but the scales' good internal reliability suggest that the items that make up the scales measure concepts consistently; for this reason, we recommend these scales. ChalleNGe programs could consider asking cadets to complete a survey measure of this type at the beginning and end of the residential phase to assess whether cadets' thinking about citizenship has changed over the course of the residential phase; these measures also could be used to measure citizenship among program graduates.

TABLE C.1
International Association for the Evaluation of Educational Achievement Civic Education Study—Citizenship Scale

Scale Questions	Not Very Important (1)			Very Important (4)
Importance of conventional citizenship An adult who is a good citizen . . .				
votes in every election	1	2	3	4
joins a political party	1	2	3	4
knows about the country's history	1	2	3	4
follows political issues in the newspaper, on the radio, or on TV	1	2	3	4
shows respect for representatives	1	2	3	4
engages in political discussions	1	2	3	4
Importance of social movement-related citizenship An adult who is a good citizen . . .				
participates in a peaceful protest against a law believed to be unjust	1	2	3	4
participates in activities to benefit people in the community/society	1	2	3	4
takes part in activities promoting human rights	1	2	3	4
takes part in activities to protect the environment	1	2	3	4

SOURCE: Schulz and Sibberns, 2004.

AmeriCorps is a federally funded national service program administered by the Corporation for National and Community Service. It targets young people from underserved communities who have not completed college. AmeriCorps includes several programs with different requirements and structures, but, broadly, young people volunteer their time in exchange for a modest stipend and educational credits. The length of service ranges from three months to one year, and the service completed by volunteers depends on the type of program and the community partner.

The measures used by AmeriCorps to assess the program's effectiveness in promoting citizenship may be useful to ChalleNGe (multiple evaluations have found evidence to support the effectiveness of AmeriCorps in promoting citizenship). Table C.3 includes the questions used by AmeriCorps to measure civic and political activities during and after participation in the program.[1] These questions, which are more focused on actions that adults might take, would be most appropriate for use *after* the ChalleNGe program.

[1] Evaluations of AmeriCorps include Finlay, Flanagan, and Wray-Lake, 2011; Frumkin et al., 2009; and Ward (2013).

TABLE C.2
International Association for the Evaluation of Educational Achievement Civic Education Study—Political Action Scale

Scale Questions	I Will Certainly Not Do This			I Will Certainly Do This
Conventional political activities When you are an adult, what do you expect that you will do?				
Join a political party	1	2	3	4
Writer letters to a newspaper about social or political concerns	1	2	3	4
Be a candidate for a local or city office	1	2	3	4
Protest activities When you are an adult, what do you expect that you will do?				
Spray-paint protest slogans on walls	1	2	3	4
Block traffic as a form of protest	1	2	3	4
Occupy public buildings as a form of protest	1	2	3	4

SOURCE: Schulz and Sibberns, 2004.

Leadership and Followership

Leadership/followership is one of the eight core components of ChalleNGe. Of the multiple conceptualizations and definitions of leadership, the theory of servant leadership is perhaps the most relevant to ChalleNGe. Servant leadership is oriented toward meeting the needs of the followers, the organization, and the larger community. Servant leadership is characterized by (1) the motivation and willingness to serve others, (2) the desire to help followers to develop into their better selves, and (3) the concern toward the larger community and its well-being (Eva et al., 2019). Aspects of this concept align well with ChalleNGe's emphasis on character and standards, including the orientation toward others and community. Measuring or assessing servant leadership could be helpful as programs seek to develop leadership/followership in cadets. Several different scales exist to measure these concepts; see, e.g., Barbuto and Wheeler, 2006.

Another option is the *Youth Leadership Life Skills Development* scale, developed to evaluate 4-H programs' effectiveness in promoting leadership in adolescents and used in the context of program evaluation. The scale is more complex, in that cadets would be asked to determine how much of their leadership development was attributable to their participation in ChalleNGe (see Seevers and Dormody, 1995).

TABLE C.3
AmeriCorps Questions

Scale Questions	Never				Always
How often do you do each of the following? Would you say you do this never, not very often, sometimes, very often, or always?					
Participate in events such as community meetings, celebrations, or activities in your community	0	1	2	3	4
Join organizations that support issues that are important to you	0	1	2	3	4
Write an email to newspaper or organizations to voice your views on an issue	0	1	2	3	4
Vote in local elections	0	1	2	3	4
Try to learn as much as you can about candidates or ballot questions before voting	0	1	2	3	4
Keep informed about local or national news	0	1	2	3	4
In the last 12 months, how often have you . . .					
expressed your opinions using the internet	0	1	2	3	4
expressed your opinion through radio call-ins	0	1	2	3	4
talked to other people to persuade them to vote for a particular party or candidate	0	1	2	3	4
contacted a government official to express your opinion on a local or national issue	0	1	2	3	4
worked as a volunteer for a political party or candidate running for national, state, or local office	0	1	2	3	4

SOURCE: Frumkin et al., 2009.

Service to Community

One of ChalleNGe's goals is to instill a sense of commitment to serve in cadets. In addition to tracking the hours that cadets participate in service to community, ChalleNGe can consider measuring some of the factors that contribute to sustained service to community. There are many ways to approach measuring service to community.

A straightforward approach would be to measure prosocial attitudes.[2] While this would not provide a direct measure of service to community, adolescents who exhibit such attitudes are more likely to volunteer (e.g., Matsuba, Hart, and Atkins, 2007; Stukas, Snyder, and Clary, 2016). Table C.4 includes the relevant items from this scale (these items have been validated

2 Prosocial attitudes can be described as falling in the domain of caring, capturing "one's sense of sympathy and empathy for others and the ability to see outside one's self" (Geldhof et al., 2014).

TABLE C.4

The 5Cs of Positive Youth Development–Short Form (Caring Subscale)

How well does each of these statements describe you?	Not Well	to		Very Well
I don't feel sorry for other people when they are having problems.	1	2	3	4
When I see someone being taken advantage of, I want to help them.	1	2	3	4
It bothers me when bad things happen to good people.	1	2	3	4
It bothers me when bad things happen to any person.	1	2	3	4
When I see someone being treated unfairly, I don't feel sorry for them.	1	2	3	4
I feel sorry for other people who don't have what I have.	1	2	3	4
When I see someone being picked on, I feel sorry for them.	1	2	3	4
It makes me sad to see a person who doesn't have friends.	1	2	3	4
When I see another person who is hurt or upset, I feel sorry for them.	1	2	3	4

SOURCE: Geldhof et al., 2014.

on a sample of more than 7,700 adolescents). The scale could be used during acclimation and at the end of the residential phase to assess the extent to which cadets' endorsements of the caring characteristics change while they are in the ChalleNGe program. A discussion of these questions also could be included in ChalleNGe's classroom curriculum.

Examples of longer-term measures include the Community Service Self-Efficacy Scale—Retrospective Version (Reeb et al., 2010; see Table 1) and the YouthBuild Commitment to Serve scale (Tomberg, 2013). However, these scales have some overlap with the citizenship scales listed in Tables C.1–C.3.

APPENDIX D

Supporting Mentors

In this appendix, we present and discuss results from a pilot program aimed at increasing support for mentors.

ChalleNGe uses a *youth-initiated mentoring* approach, in which cadets are asked to nominate potential mentors from their social network. Mentors generally cannot be immediate family members of the cadet (i.e., parent, sibling), must be at least 21 years old, must be the same gender as the cadet, and must live within a reasonable distance of the cadet's home. ChalleNGe conducts background checks and delivers formal training to mentors prior to the official match. Mentors play an important role in assisting cadets' reentry into the community after they graduate from ChalleNGe (during the post-residential phase). Mentors and graduates are expected to sustain their relationship for 12 months postgraduation. They are expected to be in contact on a weekly basis and have in-person meetings at least twice a month. Although mentor-mentee relationships do not always last throughout the post-residential period, ChalleNGe program staff are available to provide support to mentors and mentees if necessary. Mentors also report cadet placement information to program staff during the post-residential phase; in this way, mentors play an important role in measuring program outcomes.

The Mentoring Pilot—Adding Communication Skills to Mentor Training

As described in the most recent annual report (Constant et al., 2020), RAND partnered with Sunburst Youth Academy to design and implement a pilot project focused on mentors. The goals of the pilot were to (1) increase mentor retention, (2) improve the mentor-mentee relationship, and (3) increase rates of mentor reporting during the post-residential phase. The pilot project focused on mentor training. RAND researchers assessed the mentor training and recommended the addition of a specific training module on communication skills. Sunburst staff added the module to the mentoring training curriculum. The module covered two topics: active listening and empathy. Activities included role plays, group discussions, and handouts.[1] Cadets attended a portion of the training with their mentors.

[1] See Constant et al., 2020, for a detailed description of the communication skills module.

Two cohorts of mentors participated in the mentoring pilot in March and August 2019. The cohorts consisted of 150 and 202 mentors, respectively. About two-thirds of the mentors were male. Most reported their relationships with the cadets as family friends, relatives, teachers, or coaches; a few were pastors or neighbors.[2]

To summarize, mentors indicated that the additional training was relevant and helpful. In particular, mentors pointed to communication tips and information on spending time with cadets as the most useful areas of the training. Mentors also indicated that they would like to receive additional information on career exploration, as well as on family relationships and emotional and behavioral issues. Such training could assist mentors in forming and maintaining strong relationships with their mentees.

Results from the Post-Residential Survey

To understand the longer-term impression of the mentor training and to assess the mentoring relationship after cadets graduate from ChalleNGe, RAND and Sunburst fielded a post-residential survey to Cohort 1 mentors. The mentors received an email invitation to complete a web-based survey three months after graduation. The survey asks mentors to report on frequency of contact with their mentees, forms of communication (e.g., in-person meeting, phone calls, emails), the mentor's confidence in supporting their mentee, frequency of applying active listening skills when communicating with the mentee, and quality of the mentor-mentee relationship. Of the 150 mentors who were sent the post-residential survey, 25 mentors completed the survey, for a response rate of 17 percent. Sunburst has set the expectation that mentors have weekly contact with their mentee during the post-residential phase. However, only four out of 25 mentors reported meeting this expectation. *Forty percent of respondents reported that they had had only one contact in the past 30 days, and 20 percent of respondents reported no contact with their mentee.* Given the low response rate to the mentor survey, contact between all mentors and mentees may be happening even less often.[3]

During site visits, staff at many ChalleNGe sites indicated that they had difficulty retaining mentors during the post-residential phase (see Constant et al., 2019). During site visits, program staff often cited lack of interest and/or commitment from mentors as the reason mentors stopped contacting program staff. When Sunburst mentors were asked about the challenges related to keeping in touch with their mentees in the post-residential survey, the most-cited challenges were "I have had difficulty reaching my mentee" (n = 8) and "My mentee is not interested in maintaining contact" (n = 2).

---

2 Six mentors from Cohort 2 did not provide any demographic information.

3 When respondents had contacts with their mentees, most met in person (60 percent), while others sent text messages (52 percent) and made phone calls (40 percent). Percentages represent the average responses over two cohorts. Mentors were presented with a checklist of potential means of communication; the mentors could select as many or as few as appropriate.

Respondents also reported on their perception of the mentoring relationship's quality. The standard measure we used to assess perception of the mentoring relationship's quality consists of 14 items (Rhodes, Schwartz, et al., 2017). Higher scores represent more-positive perception of the mentoring relationship (range from 1 to 5). Mentors reported generally positive perceptions of their relationships with mentees (see Figure D.1). Similar ratings were recorded in another study examining the quality of the mentoring relationship between college student mentors and adolescent mentees (Weiler, Boat, and Haddock, 2019). Sunburst mentors were especially likely to report feeling close to their mentees and confident in handling the challenges of being a mentor. However, mentors reported that the time commitment of being a mentor was more than they had anticipated. The findings suggest that mentors in general enjoyed being a mentor and felt confidence in their role, but barriers such as lack of time might be negatively affecting the quality of the mentoring relationship.

Lessons Learned

The program's design assumes that mentors will play a significant role in supporting cadets during and after ChalleNGe. For some cadets, the mentoring relationship may be one of the few stable and positive relationships they have with an adult. The purpose of the mentoring pilot was to improve communication between mentors and mentees and, hopefully, to improve mentor retention and reporting. The added communication skills module was well received by both cohorts of mentors.

FIGURE D.1

Quality of Mentoring Relationship

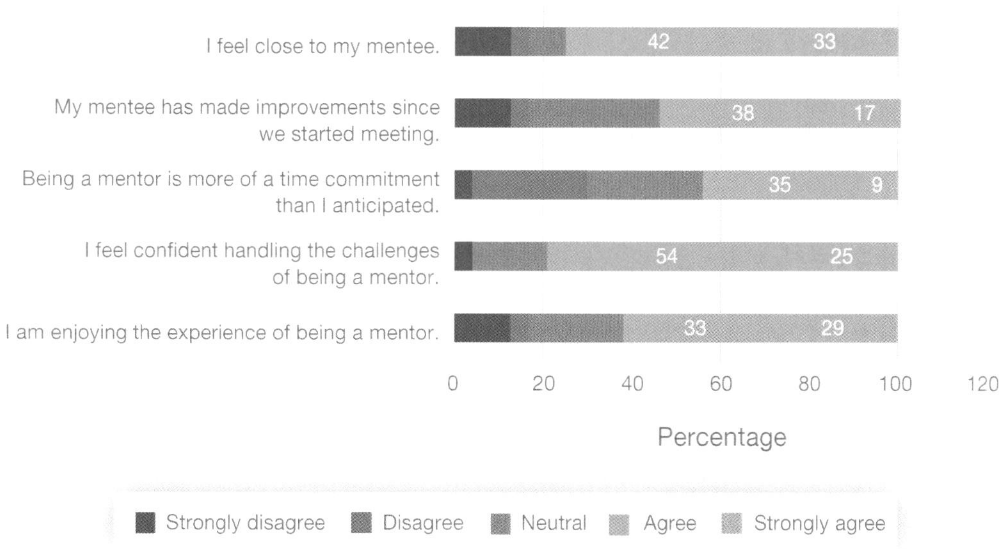

SOURCE: Three-month post-residential mentor survey.

It is difficult to draw any conclusions about the influence of the additional training on mentor retention and the mentoring relationship during the post-residential phase, given the low response rate of the three-month post-residential survey—and those who responded to the survey are likely to be different from their counterparts. For example, it is possible that mentors who maintain contact with their mentees are more likely to complete the survey. Furthermore, those who completed the survey may not be representative of all mentors in the program. However, the mentoring pilot has demonstrated that it is feasible to implement the communication skills module during mentor training and that the module is perceived to be useful by mentors.

Through implementing the mentoring pilot, we have learned some important lessons related to the mentoring program specifically and data collection in general.

- Introducing new mentor training materials: The pilot demonstrated that it is feasible for a ChalleNGe site to implement additional mentor training during the residential phase. Our prior work on the mentoring component found that mentor training varies across ChalleNGe sites. Providing evidence-informed training materials with the flexibility of adaptation can be helpful because staff members who oversee mentor training often have scant time and resources to identify and develop new mentor training. One topic to consider is career exploration; both cohorts of mentors who completed the posttraining survey expressed the strongest interest in learning more about how to help cadets explore and prepare for different career options.
- Rethinking the role of mentor during the post-residential phase: ChalleNGe sites rely on mentors to provide school and/or job placement data on cadets during the post-residential phase. The limited data collected during the three-month post-residential survey suggest that mentors have a hard time getting in touch with their mentees. If mentors are not in contact with their mentees, they cannot serve as a reliable source for placement data. For this reason, alternatives, such as self-report data from cadets, should be considered.
- Allocating resources for data collection and tracking: One difficulty we encountered during the implementation of the mentoring pilot was that ChalleNGe staff members were already overwhelmed by their work, and it was difficult for them to take on the additional tasks of data collection and tracking. Having staff dedicated to the task of data collection is critical to collecting high-quality data. For example, calling mentors to remind them to complete the survey may increase response rates. Improving response rates is important for getting more-accurate data, which can be used to make data-driven decisions to improve the mentoring program and other components of ChalleNGe. Of course, allocating time for staff members to stay in contact with mentors could also result in increasing mentor-mentee contacts. This could have positive impacts for cadets.

APPENDIX E

Survey of Washington Youth Academy Graduates

In this appendix, we include information about the survey of WYA graduates, as well as additional information about how we analyzed the survey data.

Survey Overview

In fall 2018, WYA hosted an event to celebrate the site's tenth anniversary. Staff publicized the event widely and invited former cadets to return to WYA for the celebration. Concurrently, staff publicized their alumni survey. The survey could be completed online (on a computer or a smartphone); paper copies of the survey were also available at the celebration. Figure E.1

FIGURE E.1
Washington Youth Academy Alumni Survey: Advertising

SOURCE: Images provided by WYA staff.

includes some of the advertising developed by WYA staff. To incentivize survey participation, those who took the survey received a WYA water bottle. More than 420 alumni started the survey (not all who took the survey completed each question).

Survey Administration

With input from RAND researchers, the WYA staff designed and fielded a short online survey. The survey was advertised on the site's Facebook page, through targeted emails inviting former cadets to the anniversary celebration, and in person at the site during the celebration. Participants could complete the survey online (via computer or smartphone) or on paper while attending the anniversary celebration. Former cadets who completed the survey during the celebration received a WYA water bottle. Fielding the survey through surveymonkey.com required only modest amounts of staff time and effort. The survey included questions about educational attainment, earnings and benefits, military service, family formation, and reflections on time spent at WYA. Four hundred twenty-one (421) people began the survey, although not all participants completed every question (at the time of the survey, roughly 2,500 young people had graduated from WYA). Nearly all who began the survey answered key questions (414 people).

While the survey requested the former cadets' names, no personally identifiable information was passed to RAND. Instead, program staff placed a nonidentifying individual code on the survey results; staff planned to match the surveys to their administrative database by name and class and then provide RAND researchers with the completed surveys, linked to administrative information. It is worth noting that this required substantially more effort on the part of the program staff than actually fielding the survey; also, because the administrative files were not standardized over the life of the program, accessible files covered a relatively limited period of the program's history. Therefore, many surveys could not be matched to administrative data (discussed in more detail later in this appendix). WYA staff securely transmitted the survey and administrative data to RAND staff; RAND staff completed the analyses.

To limit the amount of time required to complete the survey, the survey questions did not inquire about some basic descriptive information (such as gender and age). Staff planned to obtain this information, as well as detailed information on cadet test scores, placements, etc. from administrative files. However, matching limitations meant that such information could not, in most cases, be merged with survey responses. This is not a problem with the methodology per se, but this experience suggests that including some basic descriptive information on future surveys is preferable, even though additional questions will lengthen the time to complete the survey. Indeed, with more descriptive information, matching between survey respondents and administrative files could be possible even without a unique identifier.[1]

The most recent alumni made up a large group of the survey respondents, but respondents spanned the program history (see Figure E.2). In fact, response rates were not very different among more- and less-recent alumni. The program opened in 2009, and class size has trended upward somewhat over the years of operation. By the end of 2018, the program had graduated nearly 2,500 cadets in total. To compare more- and less-recent classes, we divided the data. Between 2009 and 2014, the program had 1,155 graduates, and between 2015 and 2018, the program had 1,313 graduates. Based on the numbers of respondents shown in Figure E.2, the average response rate among earlier cohorts (2009–2014) was roughly 16 percent, and the response rate among more recent cohorts (2015–2019) was roughly 19 percent. WYA runs two classes per year; response rates between the spring and fall classes were nearly identical.

FIGURE E.2

Washington Youth Academy Alumni Survey: Number of Respondents, by Year of Graduation

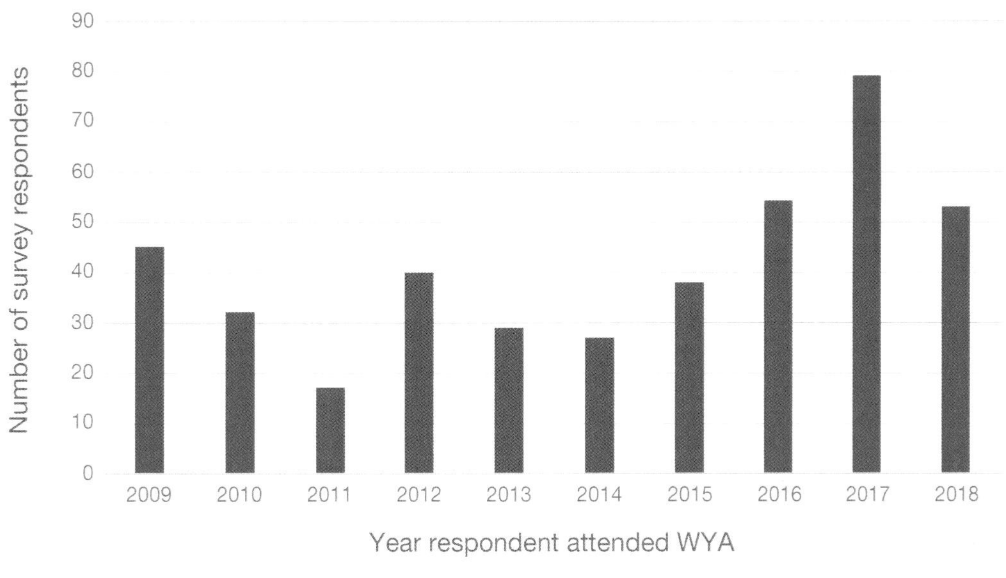

SOURCE: RAND calculations from WYA alumni survey, collected in November 2018. Number of observations: 414. Results are unweighted to demonstrate distribution of classes among respondents. Examining only those who could be included in the weighted sample produced very similar results.

[1] For example, many survey respondents could likely be matched to administrative files based on a combination of information: home ZIP code at entry, platoon, gender, month and year, etc. Future efforts should experiment to determine the minimal amount of information required for a reasonably accurate match.

Findings from the Alumni Survey

Table E.1 presents a description of the survey responses. As indicated above, survey respondents do not include all alumni, or even the majority; less than 20 percent of all WYA alumni completed the survey. This is not surprising, given the issues involved in remaining in contact with even recent graduates, and other surveys generally face similar issues.[2] For this reason, we designed survey weights to produce estimates that are more representative of all

TABLE E.1
Washington Youth Academy Alumni Survey

Measure	Weighted Mean
Number of jobs since graduation	4.2
Residence prior to entering WYA (region of Washington)	
Portland	
Seattle-Tacoma	8%
Spokane	64%
Yakima	5%
Time at current job	24%
Less than 1 year	
1–2 years	52%
2–3 years	17%
3–4 years	17%
> 4 years	9%
Job includes benefits	5%
Ever unemployed	55%
Hours worked per week	42%
Attended college	37%
Currently attending college	37%
Attending college full time (if attending now)	21%
Military service	53%
Married	9%
Have children	13%
Live with children (if have children)	22%
Live with parents	36%
Live with roommate(s)	37%
Would recommend ChalleNGe to others	13%

NOTES: 43 percent of those who attended ChalleNGe in 2016 or earlier attended college; 23 percent among those who attended ChalleNGe in 2016 or earlier. Number of observations: 367. A discussion of the weights used is presented later in this appendix.

[2] For example, see Keeter et al., 2017, for a comparison of response rates across telephone surveys, web-based surveys, and other types of surveys, all of which generally have response rates below 10 percent. The authors point out that response rates are much higher among household-level surveys with multiple methods of contact (such as the American Community Survey) but that telephone or web-based surveys still produce accurate estimates of many measures.

WYA alumni; we applied these weights to the results in Table E.1 and to the rest of the results in this section, except where noted.[3]

About 90 percent of respondents reported that they were employed when they filled out the survey; on average, they worked about 37 hours per week (nearly full time). Many respondents reported having less than one year of experience at their current jobs—this may reflect the fact that many of the respondents are still quite young (as shown in Figure E.2, about 45 percent of respondents completed WYA in the three years prior to the survey). The majority reported that their jobs included some benefits—paid time off, health insurance, or access to a retirement plan. More than one-third had attended college at some point; more than 20 percent were enrolled when they filled out the survey (and the majority of those reported attending on a full-time basis).

Respondents lived all across Washington state before entering ChalleNGe but were more likely to have lived near the site (in the Seattle-Tacoma area); nearly two-thirds of those who completed the survey reported living in the Seattle-Tacoma area.[4] Among those respondents who provided complete ZIP code information, more than half reported living in the same ZIP code as they lived in prior to entering ChalleNGe.[5] This could indicate low mobility or a pattern of moving away and then returning to one's former hometown, or it could be their relative youth.

The WYA awards high school credits to cadets; most transfer back to their home high school to work toward completing a diploma. Figure E.3 shows the reported high school graduation rate among those who completed the relevant section of the survey (solid blue line). This is the rate at which WYA graduates earned a traditional high school diploma. We plot these data by the year the alumni graduated from ChalleNGe. Across the sample, about 73 percent of respondents indicated that they had completed high school. However, as shown in Figure E.2, many of the survey respondents completed WYA within the two or three years prior to taking the survey. Therefore, many respondents had not yet had time to complete high school when they filled out the survey. Indeed, as shown in Figure E.3, only 10 percent of those who completed ChalleNGe in 2018 reported having graduated from high school by the fall of 2018 (the time of the survey). This is not surprising given that the 2018 alumni who filled out the survey left WYA in the summer of 2018 and, thus, had not yet had time to complete even a full semester at their home high schools. Because the survey included information on the time to high school graduation, we can predict graduation rates of the most recent cohorts.

In Figure E.3, we also present this *predicted* graduation rate. This rate assumes that recent WYA graduates will complete high school at the same rate and time as earlier cohorts. The

[3] We discuss our weighting methodology in more detail in the next section of this appendix.

[4] About 55 percent of the state's population lives in this area.

[5] This could be an overcount if alumni did not remember their earlier ZIP codes and chose instead to substitute their current ZIP codes. But we expect this effect to be small because alumni were somewhat more likely to include their ZIP code at the time they entered ChalleNGe than their current ZIP code.

FIGURE E.3
Washington Youth Academy Alumni Survey: High School Graduation Rates (actual and predicted)

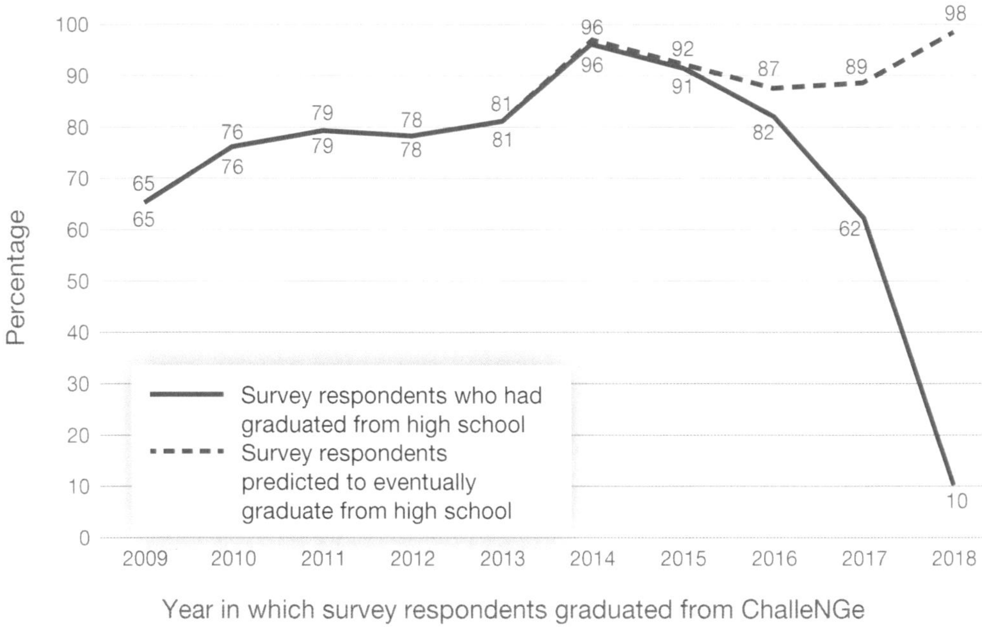

SOURCE: RAND calculations from WYA alumni survey, collected in November 2018. Number of observations: 349. Results are weighted.

survey results indicated that about 60 percent of WYA alumni who graduated from high school did so within about a year of leaving WYA. One-quarter required two years to complete high school, and another 4 percent completed high school three years after leaving WYA. Finally, a very small number completed high school four to five years after leaving WYA. In Figure E.3, we assume that recent cohorts will eventually complete high school at the same rate and in the same time frame as earlier cohorts.[6] Using this methodology, we find that the predicted eventual high school completion rate among the most recent cohorts is quite similar to the reported rate among recent past cohorts and is higher than the rate reported by the earliest cohorts. *Based on these estimates, the overall eventual high school graduation rate among those who complete WYA is predicted to be roughly 85 percent.* In other words, roughly six of seven young people who complete WYA also go on to graduate from high school. Figure E.3 also shows that high school graduation rates appear to be lower for the earlier cohorts; among those who completed WYA in the period 2014–2018, the estimated graduation rate is 92 percent. This range of graduation rates, calculated on a group of young

[6] This may be a conservative estimate, as the high school completion rate, across the country and in Washington state, has increased in recent years (Harris et al., 2020). A similar trend is evident in the 2009–2014 period in Figure E.3.

people who initially were not on track to complete high school, suggests that WYA survey respondents report graduating from high school at rates exceeding the national high school graduation rate and exceeding the rate across Washington state.[7] *However, we note here that these results are drawn from a minority of all graduates; those with more positive experiences may have been more willing than others to complete the survey.*

Labor force outcomes, including earnings, were another focus of the survey. The survey asked specific questions about the total number of jobs held since leaving ChalleNGe, periods of unemployment, hourly wages, benefits, and military service. Nearly all WYA graduates reported having held a job since leaving WYA—and more than 90 percent of the sample reported that they currently had a job or had been employed recently. Of those employed, typical earnings were in the range of $12.01–$15.00 per hour (see Figure E.4). However, nearly 30 percent reported earning less than $12.01 per hour, and nearly 40 percent reported earning

FIGURE E.4
Washington Youth Academy Alumni Survey: Hourly Earnings

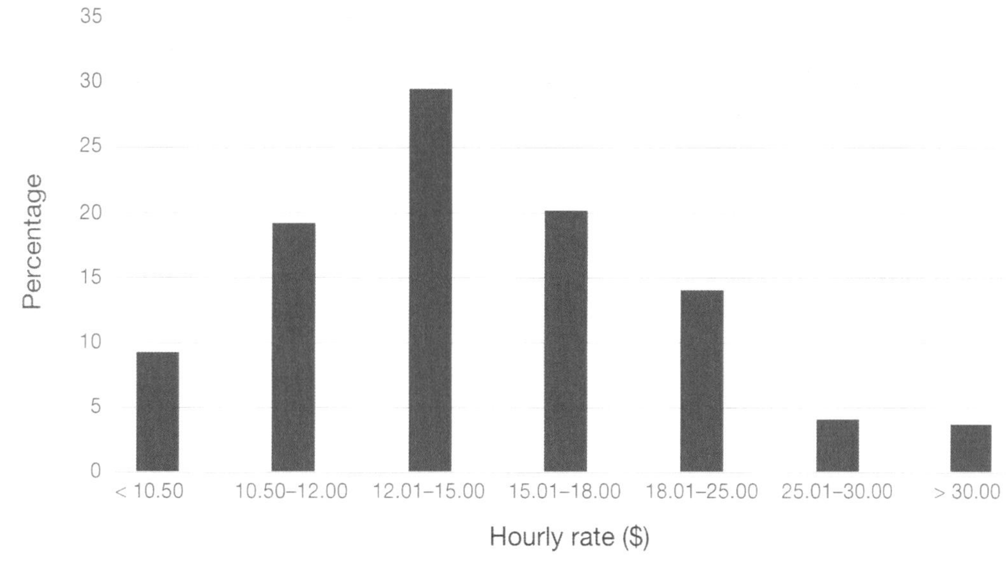

SOURCE: RAND calculations from WYA alumni survey, collected in November 2018. Number of observations: 349. Results are weighted.

[7] For a measure of national and state rates, measured by ACGR, see National Center for Education Statistics, 2020. Cadets in the earlier ChalleNGe RCT form another point of comparison. Three years after entering ChalleNGe, 30 percent of these cadets had earned a high school diploma. See Millenky et al., 2011, p. ES-6. Note that the RCT group was an *intent to treat* sample; therefore, the sample includes cadets who did not complete ChalleNGe. But the graduation (program completion) rate at WYA during recent years has exceeded 80 percent; therefore, even if we assume that none of the nongraduates completed high school, the WYA outcome compares positively with that of the group that was used to establish ChalleNGe's cost-effectiveness.

more than $15.00 per hour. In general, earnings were higher among those who were older—wages were about 6 percent higher for each additional year since completing WYA.

Survey respondents also reported usual weekly hours; about 15 percent reported that they usually worked 20 or fewer hours per week. More than 60 percent reported working 21 to 40 hours per week, and 22 percent of alumni reported that they usually worked over 40 hours per week.[8] Nearly 40 percent reported working exactly 40 hours per week, suggesting that full-time employment is not unusual. An encouraging sign is that more than half reported that their current job provided some benefits (such as health insurance, a retirement account, or paid vacation days). More than 40 percent of alumni reported that they had experienced unemployment at some point since leaving WYA, an experience normal among young workers (see, e.g., Edwards, 2020).

Survey respondents reported that they had held, on average, just over four jobs since leaving ChalleNGe. Those who graduated in earlier years reported holding more jobs, but recent graduates have held more jobs per year than earlier graduates. A likely interpretation of this result is that job stability increases over time. Still, among those in the labor force, more than half had held their current jobs for no more than one year.

At the time of the survey, those who had attended college did *not* have appreciably higher earnings than others; this likely reflects the fact that those who are enrolled in school have less time to work and less flexibility in terms of the jobs they can accept. (Also, the survey asked alumni to choose an hourly pay range, so small differences between groups may not be apparent from the survey results). We recommend continuing to track long-term earnings and to collect more-detailed information about college attendance in future surveys.

The survey asked alumni to describe their current jobs. We analyzed the free-form text responses, sorting them into standard industry classifications. Figure E.5 shows the distribution of industries among survey respondents, among 16-to-24-year-old workers, and, finally, among all workers.

In general, WYA alumni work in many of the same industries as other young workers. WYA alumni are more likely to work in the construction industry and less likely to work in professional, scientific, and technical services than other young workers (the latter may reflect the educational requirements in this industry). Finally, WYA alumni are less likely than other young workers to be employed in a series of relatively small industries listed as "Other" in Figure E.5. But, in general, WYA alumni work across many industries and are about as likely to be employed in many areas as other young workers. In particular, there is no indication that WYA alumni are more likely than others to work in the accommodation or food service industries.

Finally, the alumni survey asked respondents to reflect on how their lives had changed as a result of attending WYA; the survey also asked whether respondents would recommend the program to "a young person struggling in school." Nearly every person who completed the survey indicated willingness to recommend WYA. Their responses on how their lives

[8] The survey queried total hours; those working multiple jobs reported the total number of hours worked.

FIGURE E.5

Washington Youth Academy Alumni Survey: Employment, by Industry (compared with all U.S. workers)

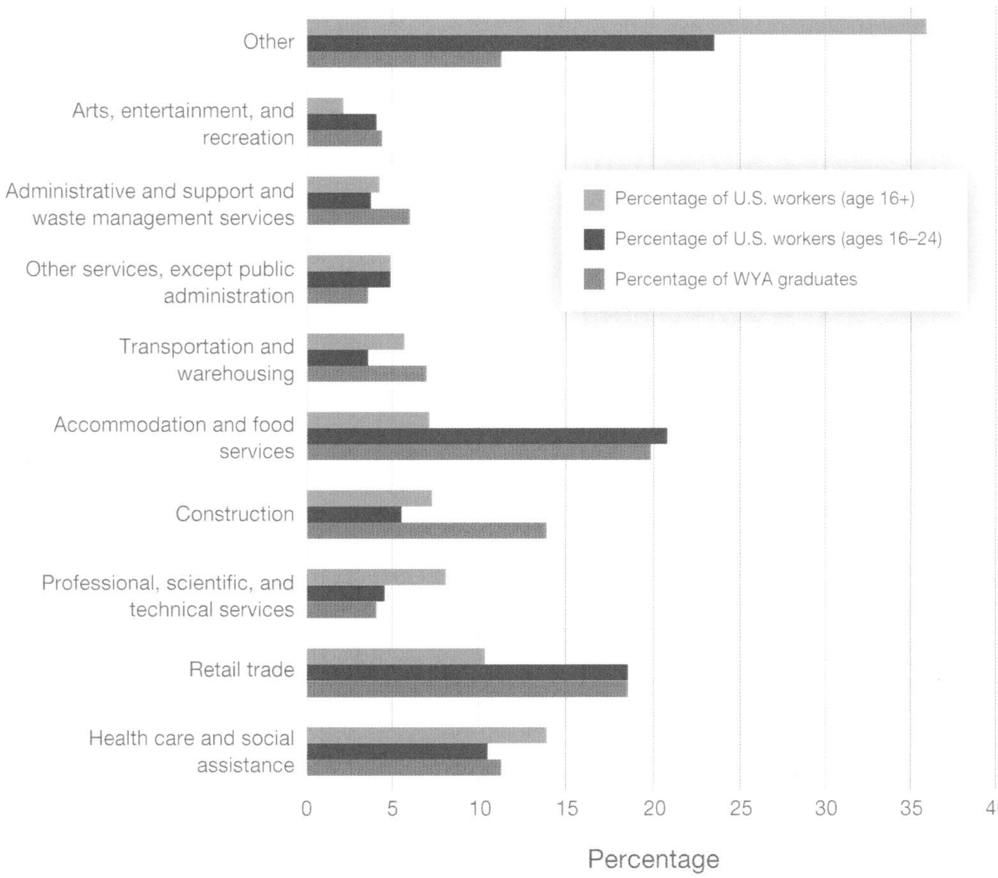

SOURCES: RAND calculations from WYA alumni survey, collected in November 2018; BLS, 2018. Number of observations: 421. "Other" category includes agriculture, forestry, fishing, and hunting; manufacturing; finance and insurance; real estate and rental/leasing; educational services; information; public administration; wholesale trade; and utilities.

had changed indicated that the program had a very positive effect on participants over a broad range of outcomes. Multiple alumni mentioned the structure and discipline, as well as the support from cadre, other staff, and other cadets. Finally, several alumni specifically mentioned their perception that, without this program, they would have died or been sent to prison at a very young age.

Analytic Methodology and Weighting Procedures

Weighting is necessary in cases in which a subsample (such as a group of survey respondents) may not be random, and evaluators desire to have the sample be representative of a larger population. If program staff had been able to select and survey a random subsample of WYA graduates (and to ensure that the entire subsample completed the survey), then the survey responses would be considered representative of all graduates of the program. However, even in cases when survey response rates are quite high, concerns about representativeness exist. Survey weights provide a solution to this potential problem (see, e.g., Cochran, 1977). The basic reason behind weighting survey responses is that different groups are differentially likely to answer the survey and are likely to answer questions differently, on average, leading to statistics biased toward the overrepresented groups if no adjustments are made. For example, in the case of the WYA anniversary celebration, it seems likely that former cadets who have had especially positive outcomes might be more likely to attend the celebration and more likely to complete the survey. The same would be likely of former cadets who live near the site. Both types of *sample selection* could mean that those who do not complete the survey would have provided somewhat different answers than those who did complete the survey. Survey weights allow a rebalancing of the sample *on the observables* by correcting overrepresentation.

Of course, the effectiveness of weighting is inherently limited by who responds to the survey and what data are known about them. Consider a simple example of weighting, in which we survey a group of 100 people, 40 of whom are women and 60 of whom are men. Our survey seeks to measure the average hourly wage; among this group, women earn $20 per hour and men earn $15 per hour. In this case, the average wage is $17. If 20 men and no women respond to the survey, the average wage reported with be $15 per hour, and weighting cannot create a response that is representative of the sample. However, if ten women and 30 men respond, the unweighted average wage would be $16.25—but, in this case, weights can be used to correct for the difference in response rates; because women were half as likely as men to respond, women's responses would be weighted twice as much as men's, and this would produce an (accurate) estimate of $17 per hour. In contrast, if 30 men and 30 women respond, weights can be used to decrease the influence of the women's responses, again producing an (accurate) estimate of $17 per hour. Another problem would be created if gender were not included in the same data, because then it could not be observed as unrepresentative and could not be corrected. However, at times, there could be a set of variables correlated with the missing variable that could stand in the place of the missing data. In the example above, years out of the labor force, education, and occupation could help control for the gender differences.

If unobservable or difficult-to-measure characteristics (such as motivation) influence both the probability of responding to a survey *and* the survey responses, then weights may still produce results that do not reflect the true measure across the population. This is again why weighting on multiple characteristics is a good idea to reduce the likelihood of sample response bias (Pfeffermann, 1993). In the case of the WYA alumni survey, we designed survey weights based on region of the state, year of attendance, and class (January versus July start).[9]

Figure E.6 provides some background on the distribution of alumni who completed the survey and demonstrates how the weights work. The lighter blue (unweighted) bars indicate the distribution of those surveyed across the four regions of Washington state.[10] The dark blue bars indicate the distribution of all WYA cadets (from the program's administrative files). The program is in the Seattle-Tacoma region; this region is also the most populous in the state. But even with these factors, alumni who lived in the Seattle-Tacoma region prior to entering WYA were more likely than others to complete the survey. The yellow (weighted) bars demonstrate that after the weights are applied, the regional distribution of the survey

FIGURE E.6

Weighting of Washington Youth Academy Alumni Survey: Region

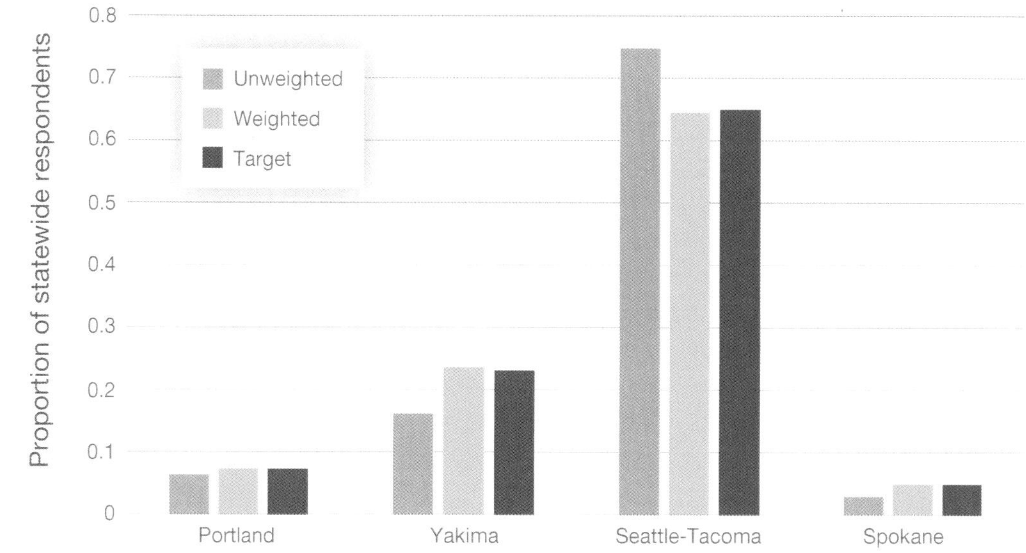

SOURCE: RAND calculations from WYA alumni survey and administrative files. Number of survey observations: 414.

---

9 We developed several different weights using a *raking* algorithm; we designed the weights based on nonidentifiable information on all WYA graduates provided by the site. Essentially, the algorithm creates weights to ensure that the survey sample resembles all WYA graduates on the selected characteristics. We selected the weights that were based on region of the state, year of attendance, and class. In this case, the weights had the effect of diminishing the relative size of the recent cohorts and of cadets who lived near the site (the most recent cohorts and those who lived nearby were more likely than other cadets to complete the survey). We experimented with weights that also used gender and TABE scores; these weights were based on a smaller sample because this information was not available for all cohorts or for all respondents. Nonetheless, these weights produced results that were generally quite similar to the results reported above. For more information about raking algorithms, see Valliant and Dever, 2018.

10 Together, these regions include the entire state. The regions are based on Washington's combined statistical areas. For more information on combined statistical areas, see U.S. Census Bureau, 2021.

respondents is quite close to the regional distribution of all cadets (the yellow bars are roughly the same heights as the dark blue bars). Thus, weighting the survey responses ensures that the sample more closely resembles the distribution of all cadets, in terms of the weighted characteristics. This methodology cannot help with sample selection that stems from unmeasured variables, such as the extent to which the participant had a positive experience at the program.

Washington Youth Academy Survey Questions

Below we present the ten survey questions administered to alumni of WYA. Names of respondents were not provided to RAND.

1. What is your name?
2. WYA class attended? (Provided as dropdown menu options; e.g., 2013-1)
3. When you entered WYA, what was your ZIP code?
4. Have you completed high school? (Y/N)
   a. If so, when did you graduate? (Year)
   b. If you graduated from a different high school than the one you attended before entering WYA, please provide the name of the high school from which you graduated: _______
   c. Have you attended college or community college? (Y/N)
   d. Are you currently enrolled in college or community college? (Y/N)
      i. Are you enrolled full-time or part-time? (1 Full-time, 2 Part-time)
5. Employment:
   a. How many different jobs for pay did you have between the time you left WYA and today? (Count only paid jobs lasting one month or more, including paid apprenticeships and internships. For self-employment or odd jobs, count multiple instances of the same type of work as one job.)
      i. Number of jobs for pay _______
   b. Between the time you started your first job and today, were there any periods of one month or more during which you were not working or serving in the United States military? (Do not include time you took off for vacation or sick leave). (Y/N)
   c. Now we are interested your current or most recent job in which you worked for pay. (If you have or most recently had more than one job, tell us about the one where you worked the most hours.)
      i. What is your job title?
      ii. How long have you worked at this job?
      iii. What is your best estimate of your hourly rate of pay? (Dropdown menu with: < $10.50/hour, $10.50–$12.00/hour, $12.01–$15.00/hour, $15.01–

$18.00/hour, $18.01–$25.00/hour, $25.01/hour–$30.00/hour, and more than $30.00/hour)

    iv. Approximately, how many hours per week do you work at this job?
    v. Do you receive benefits (access to health insurance, retirement account such as 401(k), scholarships or tuition reimbursement, paid vacation days)? (Y/N)

  d. Are you now serving or have you served in the military?
    i. Yes, active component
    ii. Yes, Guard/Reserve (checking this and the previous option should be allowable)

6. Family status: (check all that apply) married, have children, living with children, living with parents or other relatives
7. What is the ZIP code at your current address?
8. How is your life different as a result of attending WYA?
9. Would you recommend WYA to a young person struggling in school? (Y/N) Why/why not?
10. May we contact you again to learn more about your experiences? If so, please provide your email address or phone number for texts.

Matching the Survey to Administrative Files

Response rates are a challenge on nearly every survey; research concerns about response rates derive from the potential for survey respondents to differ in important ways from the population as a whole. If a survey is sent to a random subsample of the population and if the response rate among the subsample is nearly 100 percent, then researchers would have high confidence in the results of the survey. But in most cases, surveys are sent to a broad population—and only a fraction responds. In these cases, the validity of the results depends on the comparability between the subsample and the population. Weighting responses so that they (more closely) represent the population of interest offers a way to increase validity.

In the case of the WYA survey, the site primarily advertised the survey using social media. Slightly less than 20 percent of alumni filled out the survey; it is not clear how many alumni heard about the survey and declined to respond. RAND researchers recommended matching the survey results to the program's administrative files and then constructing survey weights so that respondents would more closely match the population of all alumni. However, matching the survey results to the site's administrative files was nontrivial for several reasons. First, WYA does not use Cadet Tracker; for this reason, it does not have a single administrative database. A site that uses Cadet Tracker would likely have administrative data from a longer time frame available, and this would make creating weights more straightforward. Using Cadet Tracker or another similar program could also enable sites to match survey responses to administrative information by name and class. As a final alternative, sites could add cadet identification numbers to the survey data and then use those identification numbers to match survey data to administrative files. This matched sample could be used for analysis and for creation of weights. A relatively rich administrative file *could* allow for more-precise weights (although weighting on a relatively large number of characteristics generally requires a relatively large number of survey respondents to avoid problems associated with small cell sizes). A relatively rich administrative file and the capacity to match the survey to that file also would allow estimation of specific subsets of cadets; for example, such a file would allow estimation of the effects of initial or final TABE scores, initial or final physical fitness scores, performance in the classroom, or experience in cadet leadership positions on longer-term outcomes. However, even without the capacity to match surveys to administrative files, administrative files with consistent variables available over long periods allow for the creation of detailed weights.

Abbreviations

ACGR	adjusted cohort graduation rate
CR/CC	credit recovery and course choice
CTE	career and technical education
GED	General Educational Development
HiSET	High School Equivalency Test
HYCA	Hoosier Youth ChalleNGe Academy
MBYSEP	Marion Barry Youth Summer Employment Program
RCT	randomized controlled trial
ROI	return on investment
TABE	Test of Adult Basic Education
TASC	Test Assessing Secondary Completion
WIOA	Workforce and Innovation Opportunity Act
WYA	Washington Youth Academy

References

Acemoglu, Daron, "Technical Change, Inequality, and the Labor Market," *Journal of Economic Literature*, Vol. 40, No. 1, 2002, pp. 7–72.

Autor, David H., Frank Levy, and Richard J. Murnane, "The Skill Content of Recent Technological Change: An Empirical Exploration," *Quarterly Journal of Economics*, Vol. 118, No. 4, 2003, pp. 1279–1333.

Barbuto, John E., Jr., and Daniel W. Wheeler, "Scale Development and Construction Clarification of Servant Leadership," *Group and Organizational Management*, Vol. 31, No. 3, June 2006, pp. 300–326.

Bloom, Dan, Alissa Gardenhire-Crooks, and Conrad L. Mandsager, "Reengaging High School Dropouts: Early Results of the National Guard Youth Challenge Program Evaluation," February 2009. As of November 23, 2021:
https://ssrn.com/abstract=1356853

Bound, John, and George Johnson, "What Are the Causes of Rising Wage Inequality in the United States?" *Economic Policy Review*, Vol. 1, No. 1, 1995, pp. 9–17.

Cameron, Stephen V., and James J. Heckman, "The Nonequivalence of High School Equivalents," *Journal of Labor Economics*, Vol. 11, No. 1, Part 1, January 1993, pp. 1–47.

Chan, Wing Yi, and Thomas Trail, *Integrating Psychological Counseling into National Guard Youth ChalleNGe Programs: Insights and Recommendations from Current Practices*, Santa Monica, Calif.: RAND Corporation, RR-A271-2, 2021. As of July 29, 2021:
https://www.rand.org/pubs/research_reports/RRA271-2.html

Chief National Guard, *National Guard Youth ChalleNGe Program*, Chief National Guard Bureau Instruction 9350.01, November 15, 2015.

Cochran, William G., *Sampling Techniques*, 3rd ed., New York: John Wiley & Sons, 1977.

Coles Group, *2019 MBSYEP Independent Evaluation*, Washington, D.C.: Department of Employment Services, 2019. As of September 22, 2021:
https://does.dc.gov/sites/default/files/dc/sites/does/publication/attachments/FINAL%20DELIVERED%20REPORT%20D-2_web.pdf

College Board, *Trends in College Pricing 2019*, Princeton, N.J., November 2019. As of September 27, 2021:
https://research.collegeboard.org/pdf/trends-college-pricing-2019-full-report.pdf

Common Core of Data, "Table 1. Public High School 4-Year Adjusted Cohort Graduation Rate (ACGR), by Race/Ethnicity and Selected Demographic Characteristics for the United States, the 50 States, and the District of Columbia: School Year 2016–17," database, National Center for Education Statistics, 2018. As of September 22, 2021:
https://nces.ed.gov/ccd/tables/ACGR_RE_and_characteristics_2016-17.asp

Constant, Louay, Jennie W. Wenger, Linda Cottrell, Wing Yi Chan, and Kathryn A. Edwards, *National Guard Youth ChalleNGe: Program Progress in 2017–2018*, Santa Monica, Calif.: RAND Corporation, RR-2907-OSD, 2019. As of September 22, 2021:
https://www.rand.org/pubs/research_reports/RR2907.html

Constant, Louay, Jennie W. Wenger, Linda Cottrell, Stephani L. Wrabel, and Wing Yi Chan, *National Guard Youth ChalleNGe: Program Progress in 2018–2019*, Santa Monica, Calif.: RAND Corporation, RR-4294-OSD, 2020. As of October 13, 2021:
https://www.rand.org/pubs/research_reports/RR4294.html

Cook, Colleen, Fred Heath, and Russel L. Thompson, "A Meta-Analysis of Response Rates in Web- or Internet-Based Surveys," *Educational and Psychological Measurement*, Vol. 60, No. 6, December 2000, pp. 821–836. As of September 22, 2021:
https://www.researchgate.net/publication/247728397_A_Meta-Analysis_of_Response_Rates_in_Web-_or_Internet-Based_Survey

Corte, Colleen, and Lisa Sontag-Padilla, *Goal-Setting to Support Cadet Success: Insights and Recommendations for the National Guard Youth ChalleNGe Programs*, Santa Monica, Calif.: RAND Corporation, RR-A271-6, 2021.

Department of Defense Instruction 1025.8, *National Guard Youth Challenge Program*, March 20, 2002, superseded December 31, 2020. As of September 22, 2021:
https://www.esd.whs.mil/Portals/54/Documents/DD/issuances/dodi/102508p.pdf

Doss, Christopher J., Erin M. Fahle, Susanna Loeb, and Benjamin N. York, "More Than Just a Nudge: Supporting Kindergarten Parents with Differentiated and Personalized Text Messages," *Journal of Human Resources*, Vol. 54, No. 3, Summer 2019, pp. 567–603. As of September 22, 2021:
https://www.nber.org/papers/w24450

Durlak, Joseph A., Roger P. Weissberg, Allison B. Dymnicki, Rebecca D. Taylor, and Kriston B. Schellinger, "The Impact of Enhancing Students' Social and Emotional Learning: A Meta-Analysis of School-Based Universal Interventions," *Child Development*, Vol. 82, No. 1, 2011, pp. 405–432.

Dweck, Carol S., Gregory M. Walton, and Geoffrey L. Cohen, *Academic Tenacity: Mindsets and Skills That Promote Long-Term Learning*, Seattle, Wash.: Bill and Melinda Gates Foundation, 2014. As of September 22, 2021:
https://files.eric.ed.gov/fulltext/ED576649.pdf

Edwards, Kathryn A., *Benchmarks for Success: Expected Short- and Long-Term Outcomes of National Guard Youth ChalleNGe Participants*, Santa Monica, Calif.: RAND Corporation, RR-A271-1, 2020. As of September 22, 2021:
https://www.rand.org/pubs/research_reports/RRA271-1.html

Edwards, Kathryn A., Melanie A. Zaber, and Daniel Schwam, *What Are the Skills Required to Obtain a Good Job? An Analysis of Labor Markets, Occupational Features, and Skill Training for the Youth ChalleNGe Program*, Santa Monica, Calif.: RAND Corporation, RR-A271-3, 2022.

ETS HiSET, "States and Policymakers," webpage, 2020. As of September 22, 2021:
https://hiset.ets.org/states-policy

Eva, Nathan, Mulyadi Robin, Sen Sendjaya, Dirk van Dierendonck, and Robert C. Liden, "Servant Leadership: A Systematic Review and Call for Future Research," *Leadership Quarterly*, Vol. 30, No. 1, 2019, pp. 111–132.

Finlay, Andrea K., Constance Flanagan, and Laura Wray-Lake, "Civic Engagement Patterns and Transitions Over 8 Years: The AmeriCorps National Study," *Developmental Psychology*, Vol. 47, No. 6, 2011, p. 1728.

Frumkin, Peter, JoAnn Jastrzab, Margaret Vaaler, Adam Greeney, Robert T. Grimm Jr., Kevin Cramer, and Nathan Dietz, "Inside National Service: AmeriCorps' Impact on Participants," *Journal of Policy Analysis*, Vol. 28, No. 3, 2009, pp. 394–416.

GED Testing Services, "California: Top Policies," webpage, undated-a. As of October 1, 2021: https://ged.com/policies/california/

GED Testing Services, "Michigan: Top Policies," webpage, undated-b. As of October 1, 2021: https://ged.com/policies/michigan-2/

Geldhof, G. John, Edmond P. Bowers, Megan Kiely Mueller, Christopher M. Napolitano, Kristina Schmid Callina, and Richard M. Lerner, "Longitudinal Analysis of a Very Short Measure of Positive Youth Development," *Journal of Youth and Adolescence*, Vol. 43, No. 6, 2014, pp. 933–949.

Harris, Douglas N., Lihan Liu, Nathan Barrett, and Ruoxi Li, *Is the Rise of High School Graduation Rates Real? High-Stakes School Accountability and Strategic Behavior*, Washington, D.C.: Brown Center on Education Policy, Brookings Institution, March 2020. As of September 22, 2021:
https://www.brookings.edu/wp-content/uploads/2020/02/Is-the-Rise-in-High-School-Graduation-Rates-Real-FINAL.pdf

"High School Equivalency Assessments Comparison of Tests," webpage, TASC Test, undated. As of September 22, 2021:
http://tasctest.com/pdfs/HSE_TASC_Test_Comparison_Chart.pdf

Jepsen, Christopher, Peter Mueser, and Kenneth Troske, "Second Chance for High School Dropouts? A Regression Discontinuity Analysis of Postsecondary Educational Returns to the GED," *Journal of Labor Economics*, Vol. 35, No. S1, July 2017, pp. S273–S304.

Karp, Jeffrey A., and David Brockington, "Social Desirability and Response Validity: A Comparative Analysis of Overreporting Voter Turnout in Five Countries," *Journal of Politics*, Vol. 67, No. 3, 2014.

Katz, Lawrence F., and David Autor, "Changes in the Wage Structure and Earnings Inequality," in Orley Ashenfelter and David Card, eds., *Handbook of Labor Economics*, Vol. 3, Amsterdam: Elsevier, 1999, pp. 1463–1555.

Kawachi, Ichiro, S. V. Subramanian, and Ryan Mowat, eds., "Randomized Controlled Trials and Evidence-Based Policy: A Multidisciplinary Dialogue," *Social Science and Medicine*, Vol. 210, August 2018, pp. 1–90.

Keeter, Scott, Nick Hatley, Courtney Kennedy, and Arnold Lau, "What Low Response Rates Mean for Telephone Surveys," *Pew Research Center Methods*, Vol. 15, May 15, 2017, pp. 1–39. As of September 22, 2021:
https://www.pewresearch.org/methods/2017/05/15/what-low-response-rates-mean-for-telephone-surveys/

Knowlton, Lisa Wyatt, and Cynthia C. Phillips, *The Logic Model Guidebook: Better Strategies for Great Results*, Thousand Oaks, Calif.: Sage Publications, 2009.

Malone, Lauren D., and Jennifer R. Atkin, *Cognitive and Noncognitive Improvements Among ChalleNGe Cadets: A Survey of Seven Sites*, Arlington, Va.: Center for Naval Analyses, June 2016. As of September 22, 2021:
https://www.cna.org/CNA_files/PDF/DRM-2016-U-013175-Final.pdf

Matsuba, M. Kyle, Daniel Hart, and Robert Atkins, "Psychological and Social-Structural Influences on Commitment to Volunteering," *Journal of Research in Personality*, Vol. 41, No. 4, 2007, pp. 889–907.

McGraw-Hill Communications Team, "McGraw-Hill TASC Delivers the Most Authoritative Study Plan for the New Common Core-Aligned High School Equivalency Exam," press release, April 10, 2014. As of September 22, 2021:
https://www.mheducation.com/news-media/press-releases/mcgraw-hill-education-tasc-delivers-most-authoritative-study-plan-new-common-core.html

Millenky, Megan, Dan Bloom, Sara Muller-Ravett, and Joseph Broadus, "Staying on Course: Three-Year Results of the National Guard Youth ChalleNGe Evaluation," New York: MDRC, 2011.

National Center for Education Statistics, "High School Graduation Rates," webpage, 2019. As of September 22, 2021:
https://nces.ed.gov/fastfacts/display.asp?id=805

———, "Public High School Graduation Rates," website, updated May 2020. As of September 22, 2021:
https://nces.ed.gov/programs/coe/indicator_coi.asp

National Guard Youth ChalleNGe, homepage, undated. As of September 22, 2021:
https://ngchallenge.org/

———, *National Guard Youth ChalleNGe Program: 2015 Performance and Accountability Highlights*, Washington, D.C., December 2015. As of September 22, 2021:
https://prhome.defense.gov/Portals/52/Documents/MRA_Docs/RI/2015%20NGYCP%20Annual%20Report%20Final.pdf?ver=2018-01-30-185857-893

New Jersey Department of Education, "New Jersey Adult Education Reports," webpage, 2019. As of September 22, 2021:
https://www.nj.gov/education/adulted/resources/reports/

Oreopoulos, Philip, Marianne E. Page, and Ann Huff Stevens, "The Intergenerational Effects of Compulsory Schooling," *Journal of Labor Economics*, Vol. 24, No. 4, October 2006, pp. 729–760.

Perez-Arce, Francisco, Louay Constant, David S. Loughran, and Lynn A. Karoly, *A Cost-Benefit Analysis of the National Guard Youth ChalleNGe Program*, Santa Monica, Calif.: RAND Corporation, TR-1193-NGYF, 2012. As of September 22, 2021:
http://www.rand.org/pubs/technical_reports/TR1193.html

Pfeffermann, Danny, "The Role of Sampling Weights When Modeling Survey Data," *International Statistical Review*, Vol. 61, No. 2, August 1993, pp. 317–337.

Pollard, Michael, and Matthew D. Baird, *The RAND American Life Panel: Technical Description*, Santa Monica, Calif.: RAND Corporation, RR-1651, 2017. As of September 22, 2021:
https://www.rand.org/pubs/research_reports/RR1651.html

Price, Hugh B., *Foundations, Innovation and Social Change: A Quixotic Journey Turned Case Study*, working paper prepared during a practitioner residency, Lake Como, Italy: Rockefeller Foundation Bellagio Center, July 2010.

Public Law 93-203, Comprehensive Employment and Training Act, December 28, 1973.

Public Law 97-300, Job Training Partnership Act of 1982, October 13, 1982.

Public Law 105-220, Workforce Investment Act of 1998, August 7, 1998.

Public Law 113-128, Workforce Innovation and Opportunity Act, July 22, 2014.

Reeb, Roger N., Susan F. Folger, Stacey Langsner, Courtney Ryan, and Jake Crouse, "Self-Efficacy in Service—Learning Community Action Research: Theory, Research, and Practice," *American Journal of Community Psychology*, Vol. 46, No. 3–4, 2010, pp. 459–471.

Resnjanskij, Sven, Jens Ruhose, Simon Wiederhold, and Ludger Woessmann, "Can Mentoring Alleviate Family Disadvantage in Adolscence? A Field Experiment to Improve Labor-Market Prospects," CESifo Working Paper No. 8870, 2021. As of October 13, 2021: https://ssrn.com/abstract=3779065

Rhodes, Jean E., Sarah E. O. Schwartz, Margaret M. Willis, and Max B. Wu, "Validating a Mentoring Relationship Quality Scale: Does Match Strength Predict Match Length?" *Youth & Society*, Vol. 49, No. 4, 2017, pp. 415–437.

Rhodes, Jean E., Renée Spencer, Thomas E. Keller, Belle Liang, and Gil Noam, "A Model for the Influence of Mentoring Relationships on Youth Development," *Journal of Community Psychology*, Vol. 34, 2006, pp. 691–707.

Ronfeldt, Matthew, Susanna Loeb, and James Wyckoff, "How Teacher Turnover Harms Student Achievement," *American Educational Research Journal*, Vol. 51, No. 1, 2013, pp. 4–36.

Schulz, Wolfram, and Heiko Sibberns, *IEA Civic Education Study Technical Report*, Amsterdam: International Association for the Evaluation of Educational Achievement, 2004.

Schwartz, Sarah E., Jean E. Rhodes, Renée Spencer, and Jean B. Grossman, "Youth Initiated Mentoring: Investigating a New Approach to Working with Vulnerable Adolescents," *American Journal of Community Psychology*, Vol. 52, No. 1–2, 2013, pp. 155–169.

Seevers, B. S., and T. J. Dormody, "Measuring Leadership Life Skills Development: Precursors to Research and Evaluation," *Proceedings of the Extension Education Evaluation Topical Interest Group*, American Evaluation Association Annual Meeting, Seattle, Wash., 1995.

Shankar, Maya, "How Low-Cost Randomized Controlled Trials Can Drive Effective Social Spending," blog post, Washington, D.C.: White House, July 30, 2014. As of September 30, 2021: https://obamawhitehouse.archives.gov/blog/2014/07/30/how-low-cost-randomized-controlled-trials-can-drive-effective-social-spending

Sinclair, Mary F., Sandra L. Christenson, David L. Evelo, and Christine M. Hurley, "Dropout Prevention for Youth with Disabilities: Efficacy of a Sustained School Engagement Procedure," *Exceptional Children*, Vol. 65, No. 1, 1998, pp. 7–21.

Stukas, Arthur A., Mark Snyder, and E. Gil Clary, "Understanding and Encouraging Volunteerism and Community Involvement," *Journal of Social Psychology*, No. 156, 2016, pp. 243–255.

TABE Test, homepage, Data Recognition Corporation, undated. As of October 1, 2021: https://tabetest.com/

Thaler, Richard H., and Cass R. Sunstein, *Nudge: Improving Decisions About Health, Wealth, and Happiness*, New Haven, Conn.: Yale University Press, 2008.

Tierney, Joseph P., Jean B. Grossman, and Nancy L. Resch, *Making a Difference: An Impact Study of Big Brothers Big Sisters*, Philadelphia, Pa.: Public/Private Ventures," January 2000. As of October 13, 2021: https://www.researchgate.net/publication/242542499_Making_a_Difference_An_Impact_Study_of_Big_Brothers_Big_Sisters

Tomberg, Kathleen A., *Youth Development Through Service: A Quality Assessment of the YouthBuild AmeriCorps Program*, New York: John Jay College of Criminal Justice, January 31, 2013. As of October 14, 2021: https://academicworks.cuny.edu/jj_pubs/423/

Tüzemen, Didem, and Jonathan Willis, "The Vanishing Middle: Job Polarization and Workers' Response to the Decline in Middle-Skill Jobs," *Economic Review*, Federal Reserve Bank of Kansas City, Vol. 98, 2013, pp. 5–32.

U.S. Bureau of Labor Statistics, homepage, 2020. As of September 22, 2021: https://www.bls.gov/

———, "Current Employment Statistics," database, 2018.

U.S. Census Bureau, "Combined Statistical Areas Map (September 2018)," webpage, last revised October 8, 2021. As of October 12, 2021: https://www.census.gov/geographies/reference-maps/2018/geo/csa.html

U.S. Code, Title 32, Chapter 5, Section 509, National Guard Youth Challenge Program of Opportunities for Civilian Youth, November 18, 1997.

U.S. Department of Labor, Employment and Training Administration, *Job Corps Process Study: Final Report*, Washington, D.C.: IMPAQ International, LLC, 2014. As of October 13, 2021: https://impaqint.com/work/project-reports/job-corps-process-study-final-report

U.S. Department of Labor, Office of Job Corps, *Policy and Requirements Handbook (Chapters 1–6)*, June 15, 2021.

U.S. Department of Labor, Employment and Training Administration Advisory System, *Training and Employment Guidance Letter WIOA No. 10-16, Change 1—Operating Guidance for the Workforce Innovation and Opportunity Act (Referred to as WIOA)*, Washington, D.C., August 23, 2017. As of September 22, 2021: https://wdr.doleta.gov/directives/attach/TEGL/TEGL_10-16-Change1.pdf

Valliant, Richard, and Jill A. Dever, *Survey Weights: A Step-by-Step Guide to Calculation*, College Station, Tex.: Stata Press, 2018. As of October 14, 2021: https://www.stata-press.com/books/sw-preview.pdf

Weiler, Lindsey M., Ashley A. Boat, and S. Haddock, "Youth Risk and Mentoring Relationship Quality: The Moderating Effect of Program Experiences," *American Journal of Community Psychology*, Vol. 63, No. 1–2, 2019, pp. 73–87.

Wenger, Jennie W., Louay Constant, and Linda Cottrell, *National Guard Youth ChalleNGe: Program Progress in 2016–2017*, Santa Monica, Calif.: RAND Corporation, RR-2276-OSD, 2018. As of September 22, 2021: https://www.rand.org/pubs/research_reports/RR2276.html

Wenger, Jennie W., Louay Constant, Linda Cottrell, Jenna W. Kramer, and Stephani L. Wrabel, *National Guard Youth ChalleNGe: Program Progress in 2019–2020*, Santa Monica, Calif.: RAND Corporation, RR-A882-1, 2021. As of June 10, 2021: https://www.rand.org/pubs/research_reports/RRA882-1.html

Wenger, Jennie W., Louay Constant, Linda Cottrell, Thomas E. Trail, Michael J. D. Vermeer, and Stephani L. Wrabel, *National Guard Youth ChalleNGe: Program Progress in 2015–2016*, Santa Monica, Calif.: RAND Corporation, RR-1848-OSD, 2017. As of September 22, 2021: https://www.rand.org/pubs/research_reports/RR1848.html

Wenger, Jennie, Cathleen McHugh, Seema Sayala, and Robert Shuford, "Variation in Participants and Policies Across ChalleNGe Programs," CNA Corporation, Alexandria, Va., 2008.

Yoo, Paul Youngmin, Anamarie A. Whitaker, and Jennifer Sloan McCombs, *Putting Data to Work for Young People: A Ten-Step Guide for Expanded Learning Intermediaries*, Santa Monica, Calif.: RAND Corporation, 2019. As of October 13, 2021: https://www.rand.org/pubs/tools/TL350.html

Zinth, Jennifer, "GED, HiSET and TASC: A Comparison of High School Equivalency Assessments," Denver, Colo.: Education Commission of the States, July 2015. As of September 22, 2021: https://files.eric.ed.gov/fulltext/ED558072.pdf